AF473882

EMERGENCY EXITS

Published by IWM, Lambeth Road, London SE1 6HZ
iwm.org.uk

ISBN 978-1-9124-2397-2

A catalogue record for this book is available from the British Library
Printed and bound by Gomer Press Limited
Colour reproduction by ec2i Limited

EU Authorised Representative: EAS Europe – Mustamäe tee 50, 10621 Tallinn, Estonia, gpsr.requests@easproject.com

Front cover: Askari members of the Kenya Police Force led by a Sikh officer parade during the Kenya 'Emergency' (detail).

Back cover: Hannah Wanjikũ was sexually assaulted by a soldier during the Kenya 'Emergency' (detail).

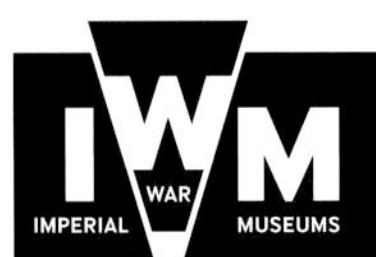

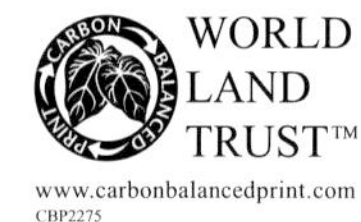

EMERGENCY EXITS

Carl Warner

INTRODUCTION

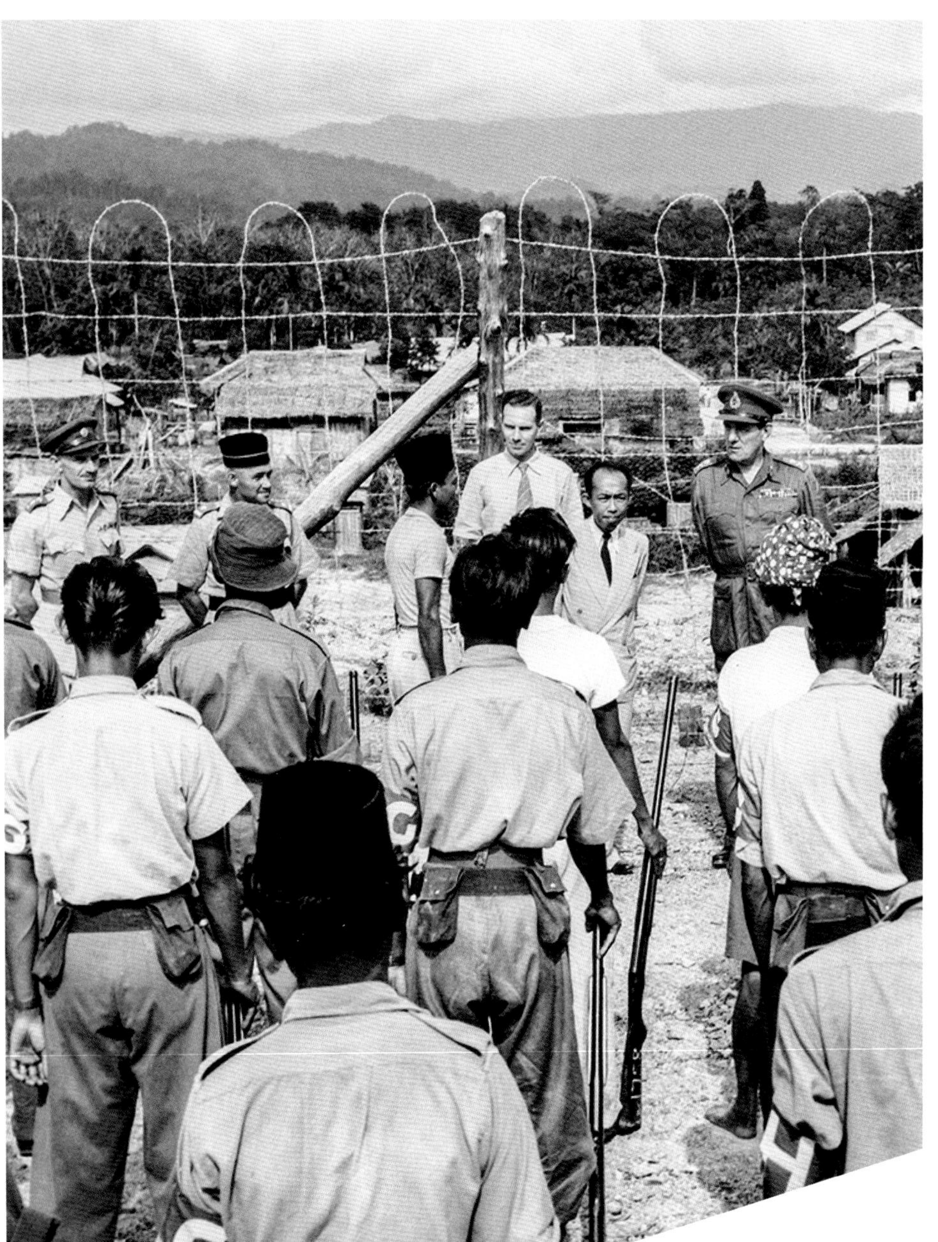

Lieutenant General Sir Geoffrey Bourne addresses Home Guard recruits. These locally-raised defence forces became a key part of the colonial campaign, but also represented deepening social and ethnic divisions within Malaya.

Within two decades of the end of the Second World War, most countries in the British Empire had gained independence. For the people of Malaya (now Malaysia), Kenya and Cyprus, and for the National Servicemen, regulars, and locally-raised troops and police who fought in the conflicts of the 1950s, the end of the British Empire was often as violent as its construction.

For centuries, the empire had provided wealth to Britain. Some territories were occupied for their resources, others for their strategic position. But empire was most often justified by ideas of racial superiority and a self-image of benevolent rule. As Cecil Rhodes declared in 1877: 'I contend that we are the finest race in the world... Just fancy those parts... inhabited by the most despicable specimens of human beings... brought under Anglo-Saxon influence.'

The Second World War weakened Europe's empires and emboldened resistance. Many colonised people had fought against fascism, only to return home to colonial rule. Imperial Japan had shattered the idea of European invincibility in Southeast Asia. New international pressures, particularly from the United States and the United Nations, amplified calls for self-determination.

But Britain, its economy damaged by war and keen to preserve its influence, was unwilling to let go entirely. Governments and colonial administrators still hoped to protect settler economies, maintain control over strategic bases, and shape a post-imperial world that would remain aligned with British interests.

Conflicts in Malaya, Kenya and Cyprus were officially labelled 'emergencies', a term that gave colonial authorities sweeping powers and allowed financial losses to be covered by insurers, unlike in declared wars.

The Malayan 'Emergency' (1948–1960) was a counter-insurgency campaign against the Malayan National Liberation

Army (MNLA), which had helped fight the Japanese during the war but now sought a communist Malaya. British forces responded to attacks on tin mines and rubber plantations with military action and mass resettlement, relocating over half a million people to government-controlled 'New Villages'.

In Kenya, the Mau Mau uprising (1952–1960), led by mainly Gikuyu, Embu and Meru people, sought to end colonial rule and reclaim land. The movement began with attacks on settler farms. In response, the British deployed troops and local forces. The conflict escalated rapidly. Over 80,000 Kenyans were detained without trial in prison camps, and hundreds of thousands more were forcibly relocated. Torture and forced labour were used in the name of 'rehabilitation'.

In Cyprus, the National Organisation of Cypriot Fighters (EOKA) fought a campaign from 1955 to 1959 for independence and union with Greece, known as *Enosis*. Cyprus was of strategic value to Britain, serving as a military base in a region of increasing Cold War significance. British forces imposed curfews, mass searches and collective punishments. Violence affected all communities, and colonial authorities stoked tension between Greek and Turkish Cypriots as part of a divide-and-rule strategy.

Across all three conflicts, Britain employed similar methods: blend conventional military force with 'hearts and minds' tactics; use intelligence networks and infrastructure control; enlist local police and troops; and separate insurgents from civilians through relocation and surveillance.

Tens of thousands died in these conflicts. The majority were civilians. Violence came from both sides. But in each case, colonial powers retained control over how the conflict was recorded and remembered.

Official records, and most of the photography in this book, reflect British perspectives. IWM's collections include a range of images but primarily contains British official photographs, taken by military and government personnel in the course of their duties. A significant number were created or distributed by the Central Office of Information (COI), the government's main public information agency. These were not neutral documents. They were part of a deliberate campaign to define the terms of each conflict, framing British forces as agents of order and progress, and their opponents as 'bandits', 'guerrillas', or 'terrorists'.

In Britain, these wars have largely faded from public memory. Unlike the two world wars, they have not been widely commemorated via regular anniversary events. British forces emerged with a reputation for restraint and counter-insurgency skill, one that would shape the way they were perceived in later conflicts.

More recently, survivors, researchers and legal advocates have forced a reckoning. Their work has uncovered thousands of hidden colonial documents and challenged long-standing narratives. This has led to greater understanding and reflection.

In 2023, King Charles III acknowledged the brutality of Britain's retreat in Kenya: 'There were abhorrent and unjustifiable acts of violence committed against Kenyans... for that, there can be no excuse.' Similar statements have been made about brutality in Malaya and Cyprus.

The photographs here tell a fraction of a huge story. They offer only brief, partial glimpses into three violent, complex conflicts that continue to shape lives today. As one journalist who served as a Royal Marine officer in Malaya stated many years later: 'War is the moral maze with an entrance but no exit – and no pretty statue to be found in the middle.'

This poster illustrates the scale of the British Empire, its administrative complexity and its economic purpose. Colonial economies were structured to extract resources through cheap, and sometimes forced, labour. During wartime, these were portrayed as shared imperial contributions. In reality, power and profit remained tightly held in British hands.

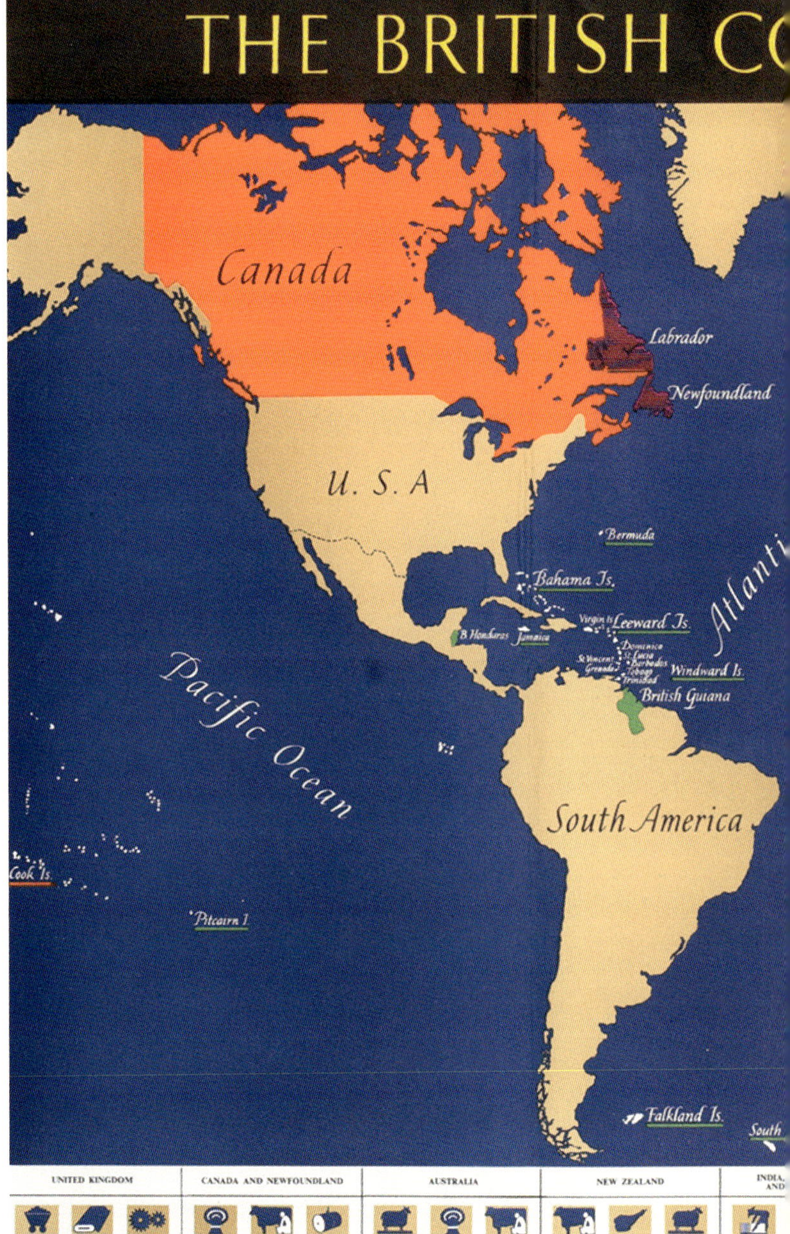

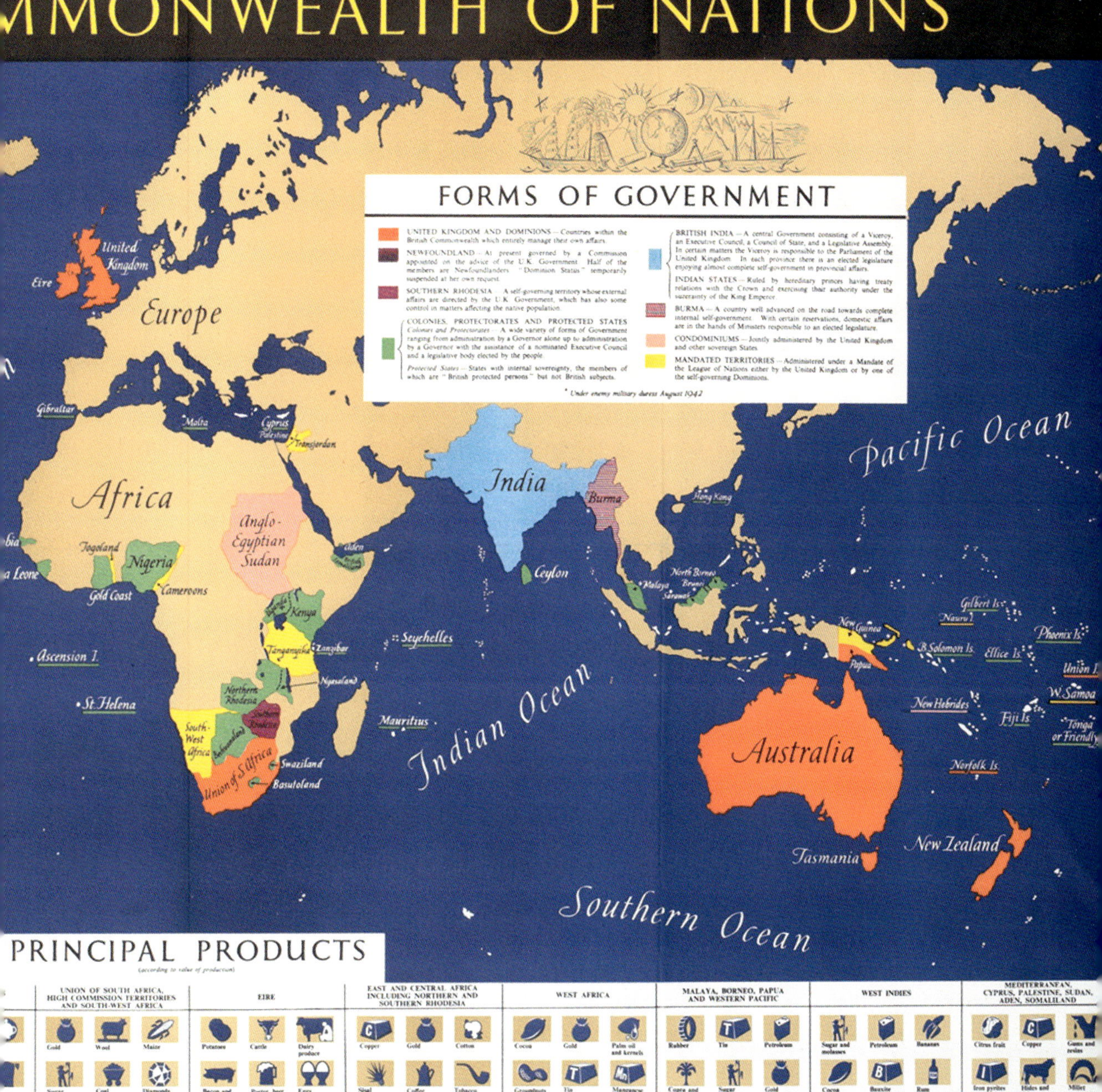
MMONWEALTH OF NATIONS
FORMS OF GOVERNMENT
UNITED KINGDOM AND DOMINIONS — Countries within the British Commonwealth which entirely manage their own affairs.
NEWFOUNDLAND — At present governed by a Commission appointed on the advice of the U.K. Government. Half of the members are Newfoundlanders. "Dominion Status" temporarily suspended at her own request.
SOUTHERN RHODESIA — A self-governing territory whose external affairs are directed by the U.K. Government, which has also some control in matters affecting the native population.
COLONIES, PROTECTORATES AND PROTECTED STATES
Colonies and Protectorates — A wide variety of forms of Government ranging from administration by a Governor alone up to administration by a Governor with the assistance of a nominated Executive Council and a legislative body elected by the people.
Protected States — States with internal sovereignty, the members of which are "British protected persons" but not British subjects.
BRITISH INDIA — A central Government consisting of a Viceroy, an Executive Council, a Council of State, and a Legislative Assembly. In certain matters the Viceroy is responsible to the Parliament of the United Kingdom. In each province there is an elected legislature enjoying almost complete self-government in provincial affairs.
INDIAN STATES — Ruled by hereditary princes having treaty relations with the Crown and exercising their authority under the suzerainty of the King Emperor.
BURMA — A country well advanced on the road towards complete internal self-government. With certain reservations, domestic affairs are in the hands of Ministers responsible to an elected legislature.
CONDOMINIUMS — Jointly administered by the United Kingdom and other sovereign States.
MANDATED TERRITORIES — Administered under a Mandate of the League of Nations either by the United Kingdom or by one of the self-governing Dominions.
* Under enemy military duress August 1942
United Kingdom
Eire
Europe
Gibraltar
Malta
Cyprus
Palestine
Transjordan
Africa
Togoland
Nigeria
Gold Coast
Cameroons
Anglo-Egyptian Sudan
Aden
Kenya
Tanganyika
Zanzibar
Nyasaland
Northern Rhodesia
Southern Rhodesia
South-West Africa
Bechuanaland
Union of S. Africa
Swaziland
Basutoland
Seychelles
Ascension I.
St. Helena
Mauritius
Indian Ocean
India
Ceylon
Burma
Hong Kong
Malaya
North Borneo
Brunei
Sarawak
New Guinea
Papua
Pacific Ocean
Gilbert Is.
Nauru I.
Phoenix Is.
B. Solomon Is.
Ellice Is.
Union I.
New Hebrides
Fiji Is.
W. Samoa
Tonga or Friendly
Norfolk Is.
Australia
Tasmania
New Zealand
Southern Ocean
PRINCIPAL PRODUCTS
(according to value of production)
UNION OF SOUTH AFRICA, HIGH COMMISSION TERRITORIES AND SOUTH-WEST AFRICA
Gold
Wool
Maize
Sugar
Coal
Diamonds
Fresh, dried & canned Fruits • Textiles • Wheat
EIRE
Potatoes
Cattle
Dairy produce
Bacon and ham
Porter, beer and ale
Eggs
Horses • Clothing, boots and shoes • Textiles
EAST AND CENTRAL AFRICA INCLUDING NORTHERN AND SOUTHERN RHODESIA
Copper
Gold
Cotton
Sisal
Coffee
Tobacco
Maize • Tea • Asbestos • Chrome
WEST AFRICA
Cocoa
Gold
Palm oil and kernels
Groundnuts
Tin
Manganese
Diamonds • Hides and skins • Iron ore • Kola
MALAYA, BORNEO, PAPUA AND WESTERN PACIFIC
Rubber
Tin
Petroleum
Copra and coconuts
Sugar
Gold
Iron ore • Phosphates • Pineapples • Timber
WEST INDIES
Sugar and molasses
Petroleum
Bananas
Cocoa
Bauxite
Rum
Mahogany • Gold • Asphalt • Arrowroot
MEDITERRANEAN, CYPRUS, PALESTINE, SUDAN, ADEN, SOMALILAND
Citrus fruit
Copper
Gums and resins
Iron pyrites
Hides and skins
Millet
Carobs • Cottonseed • Sesamum

The British Colonial Empire

ADEN
ANTIGUA
BAHAMAS
BARBADOS
BASUTOLAND
BECHUANALAND PROTECTORATE
BERMUDA
BRITISH GUIANA
BRITISH HONDURAS
BRITISH SOLOMON IS.
BRITISH VIRGIN IS.
CEYLON
CYPRUS
DOMINICA
FALKLAND IS.
FIJI
GAMBIA
GIBRALTAR
GILBERT & ELLICE IS.
GOLD COAST
GRENADA
HONG KONG
JAMAICA
KENYA

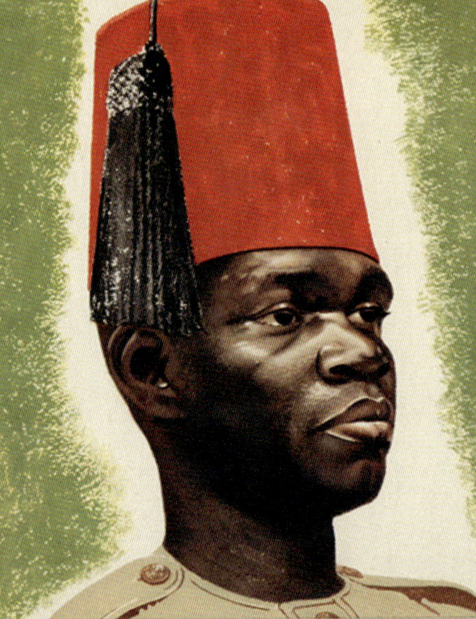

The King's African Rifles

OUR ALLIES THE COLONIES

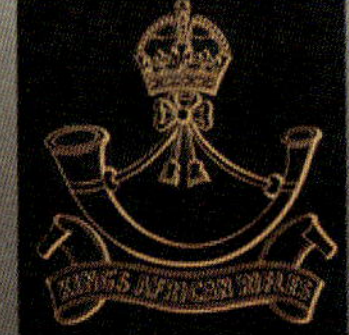

MALAYA
MALTA
MAURITIUS
MONTSERRAT
NEW HEBRIDES
NIGERIA
NORTH BORNEO
NORTHERN RHODESIA
NYASALAND
PALESTINE
ST. HELENA
ST. KITTS
ST. LUCIA
ST. VINCENT
SARAWAK
SEYCHELLES
SIERRA LEONE
SOMALILAND
SWAZILAND
TANGANYIKA
TONGA
TRANSJORDAN
TRINIDAD
UGANDA
ZANZIBAR

The British Empire was often described as a shared project, to which each nation contributed eagerly and equally. While some colonised people expressed pride in their membership, others recognised that there were deep inequalities. Many questioned whether their countries were truly being run in the interests of their people. This sense of inequality contributed to post-war calls for independence.

The surrender of Singapore in 1940 was described by British Prime Minister Winston Churchill as 'the worst disaster and the largest capitulation in British history'. Thousands of British and Allied soldiers became prisoners of war, and civilians were interned. All were brutally treated by their captors. It shattered the impression that British and other European colonial powers were invincible. In this photo, British soldiers push a car into the harbour to prevent it falling into Japanese hands.

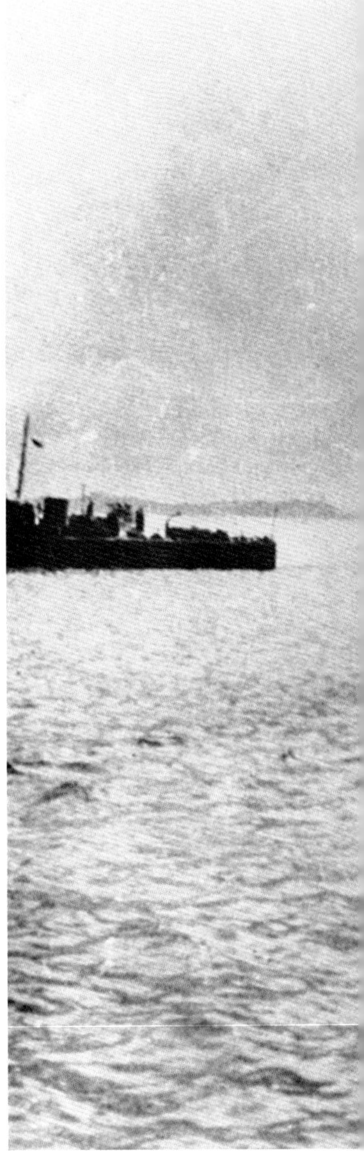

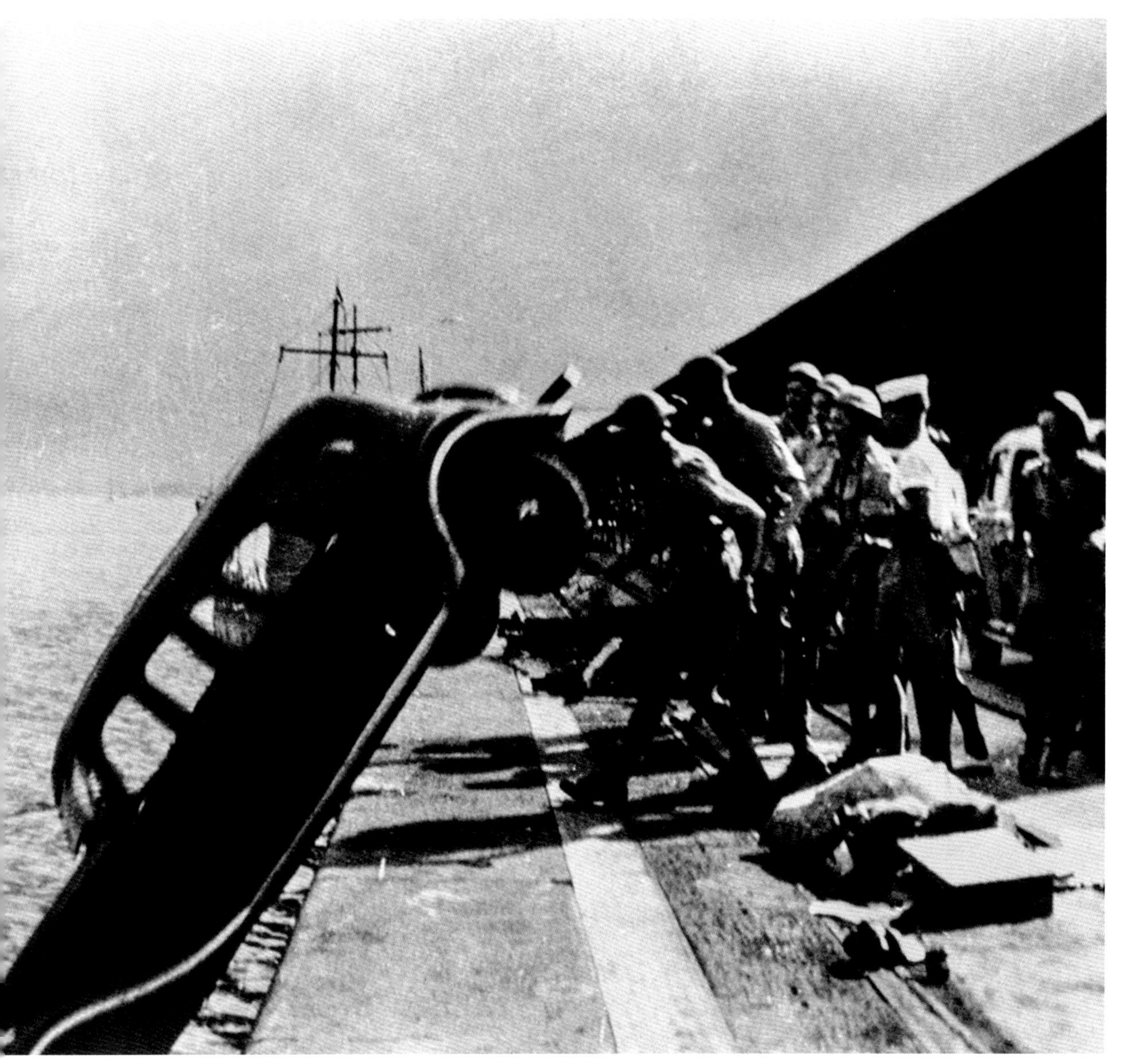

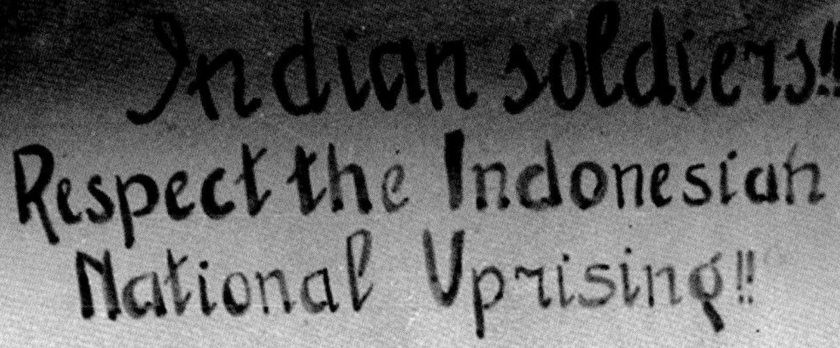
Indian soldiers!!
Respect the Indonesian
National Uprising!!
The Indonesians are fighting for freedom like you
Allahabad, September 30. Pandit Jawaharlal Nehru,
Leader of the Indian National Congress, declared
today that Indian troops must not be used to sup-
press the uprisings of the Indonesian or other colo-
nial peoples. „We are interested in the freedom of subject
countries of Asia and Africa, and we would like to help them
to achieve it," Nehru said.
„It is monstrous that our armed forces should be employed
to suppress those for whom we have the greatest sympathy.
Note:
The Indonesian people has declared her independence and is now struggling to protect it.

In 1945, Indian troops under British command were sent to Indonesia to subdue nationalist forces seeking independence from Dutch colonial rule. Officially, this was part of the regional stabilisation and Japanese surrender process. In practice, it helped re-establish Dutch control.

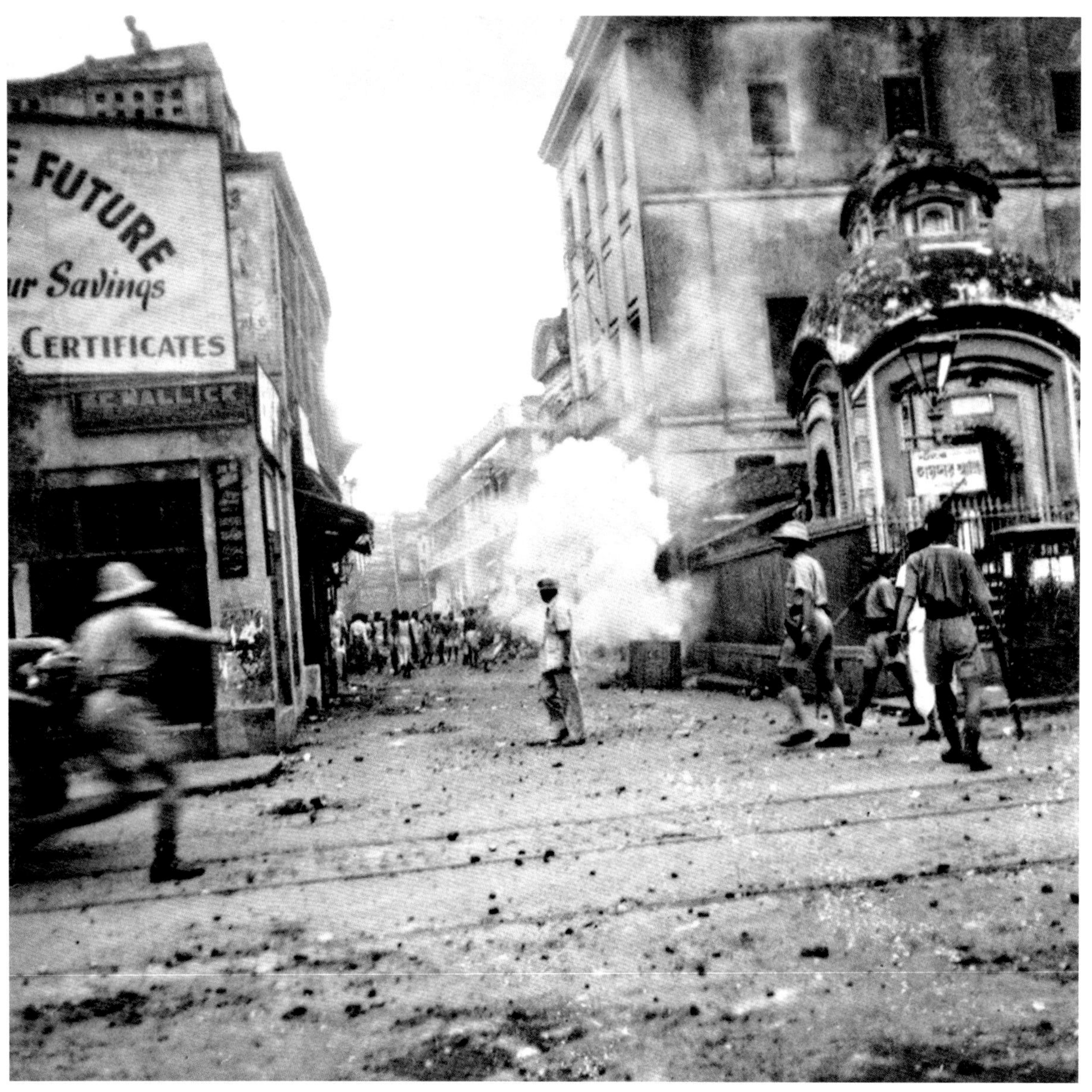
E FUTURE
ur Savings
CERTIFICATES

India and Pakistan achieved independence in 1947, but violence continued between communities during the partition. For many across the British Empire, the late 1940s were marked by turmoil, uncertainty and rising tensions between colonial aims and nationalist hopes. This photo shows devastating riots in Kolkata, India, in 1946.

In the late 1940s, Britain faced pressure to balance competing claims from Arab and Jewish groups in Mandatory Palestine, and from the international community. Violence escalated, including the bombing of infrastructure and other targets. Here the military and government HQ is attacked by the Jewish group 'Irgun'.

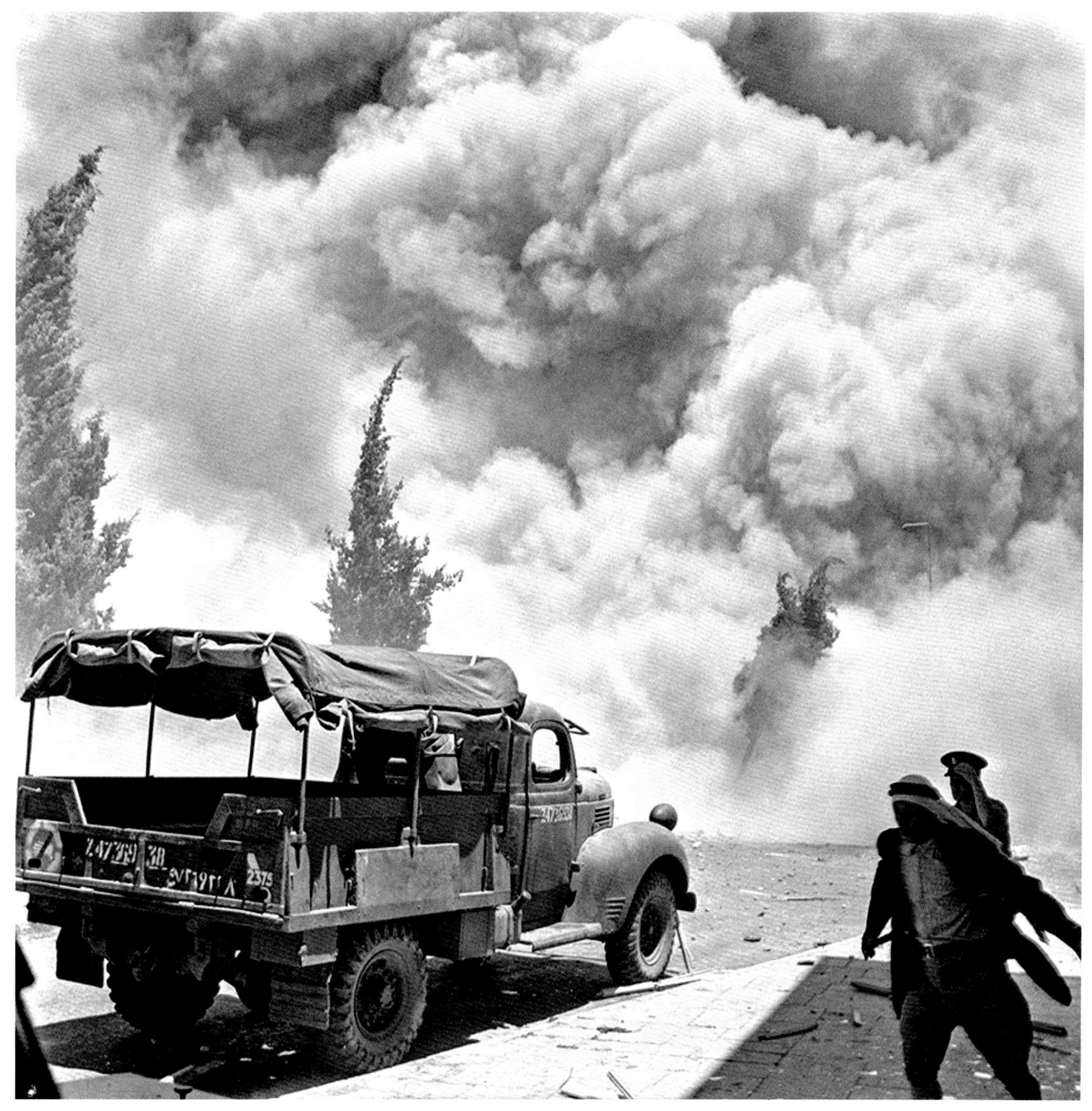

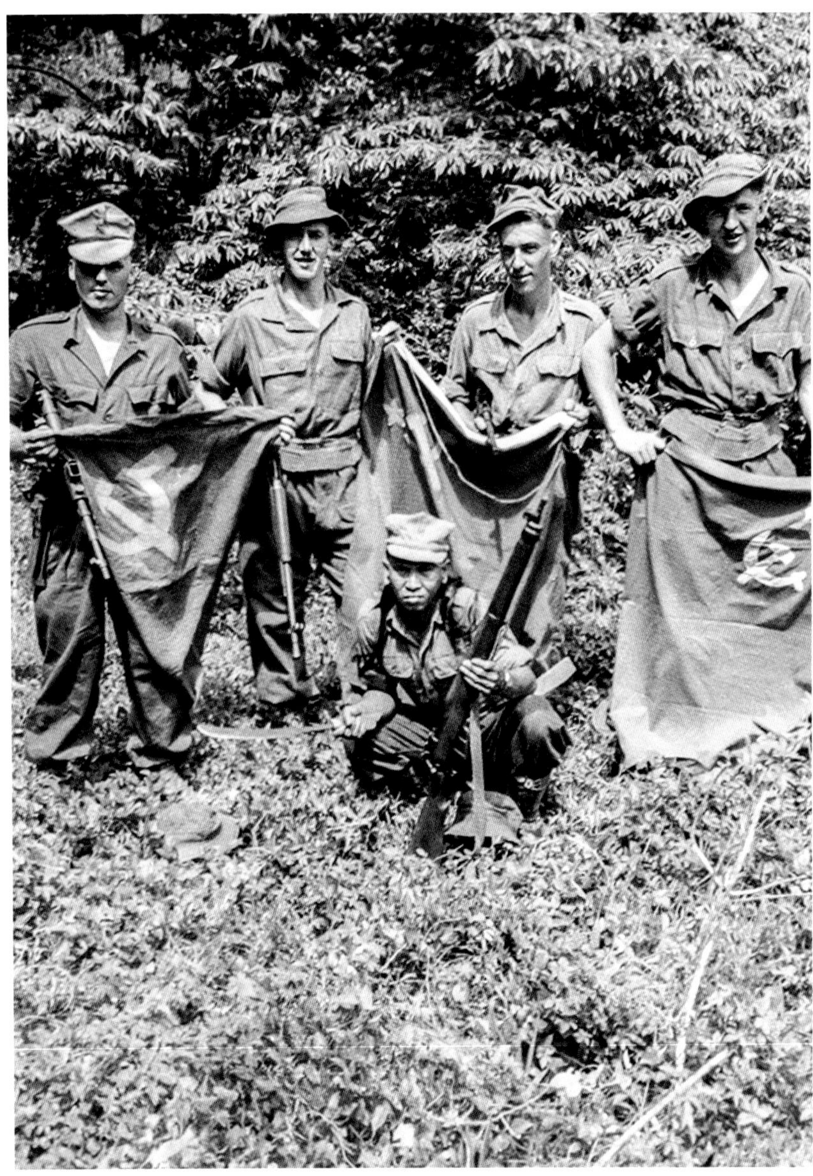

Captured Malayan National Liberation Army (MNLA) flags held by British soldiers with their local guide. The MNLA was the military part of the Malayan Communist Party. Its aims were to end British colonial rule in Malaya and replace it with a communist government. Its fighters – 10,000 active soldiers – were largely drawn from the ethnic Chinese population. Not all supporters of the MNLA were motivated by a desire for communism. Many saw this struggle as the best option for achieving independence from Britain, or to solve pressing economic and social problems.

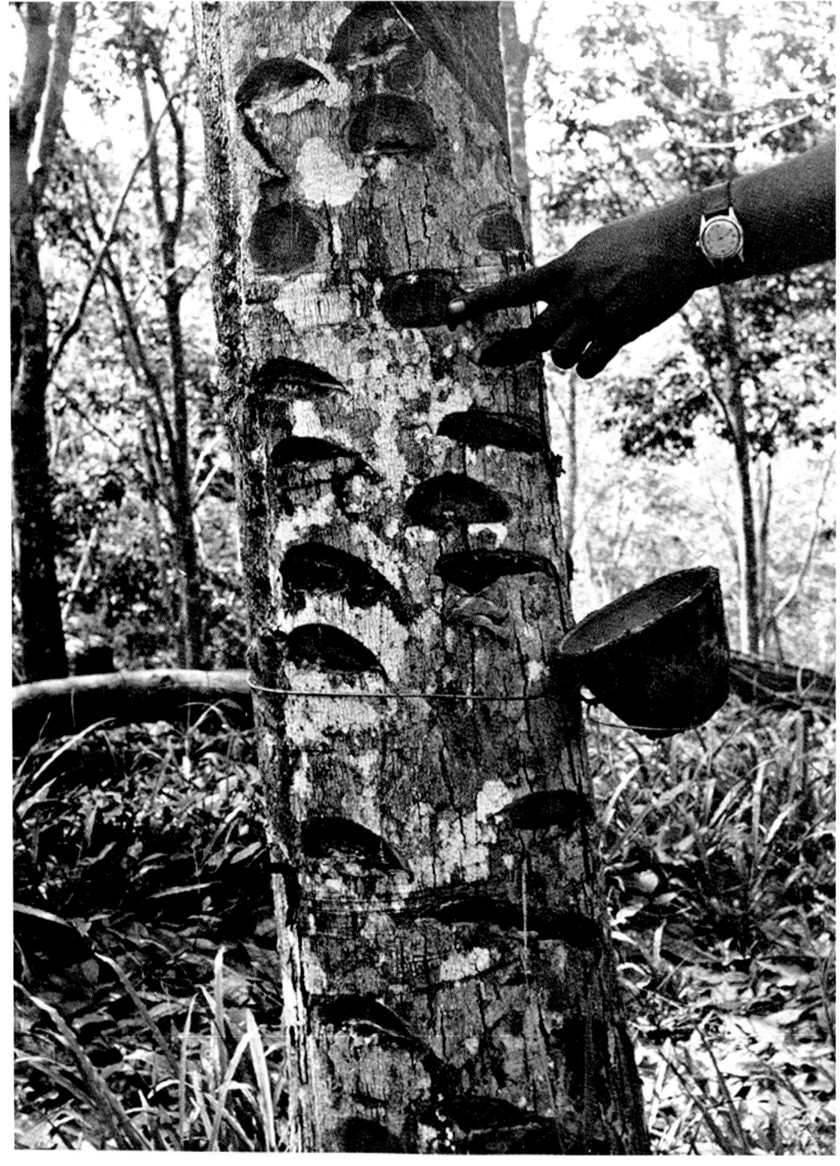

Britain's economy relied heavily on two Malayan resources: tin and rubber. One British politician noted in 1950 that the two industries 'have very largely supported the standard of living of the people of this country and the sterling area ever since the war ended; what we should do without Malaya, and its earnings in tin and rubber, I do not know.' The MNLA, too, recognised their value, and targeted them in a campaign against colonial rule. This photograph shows a damaged rubber tree.

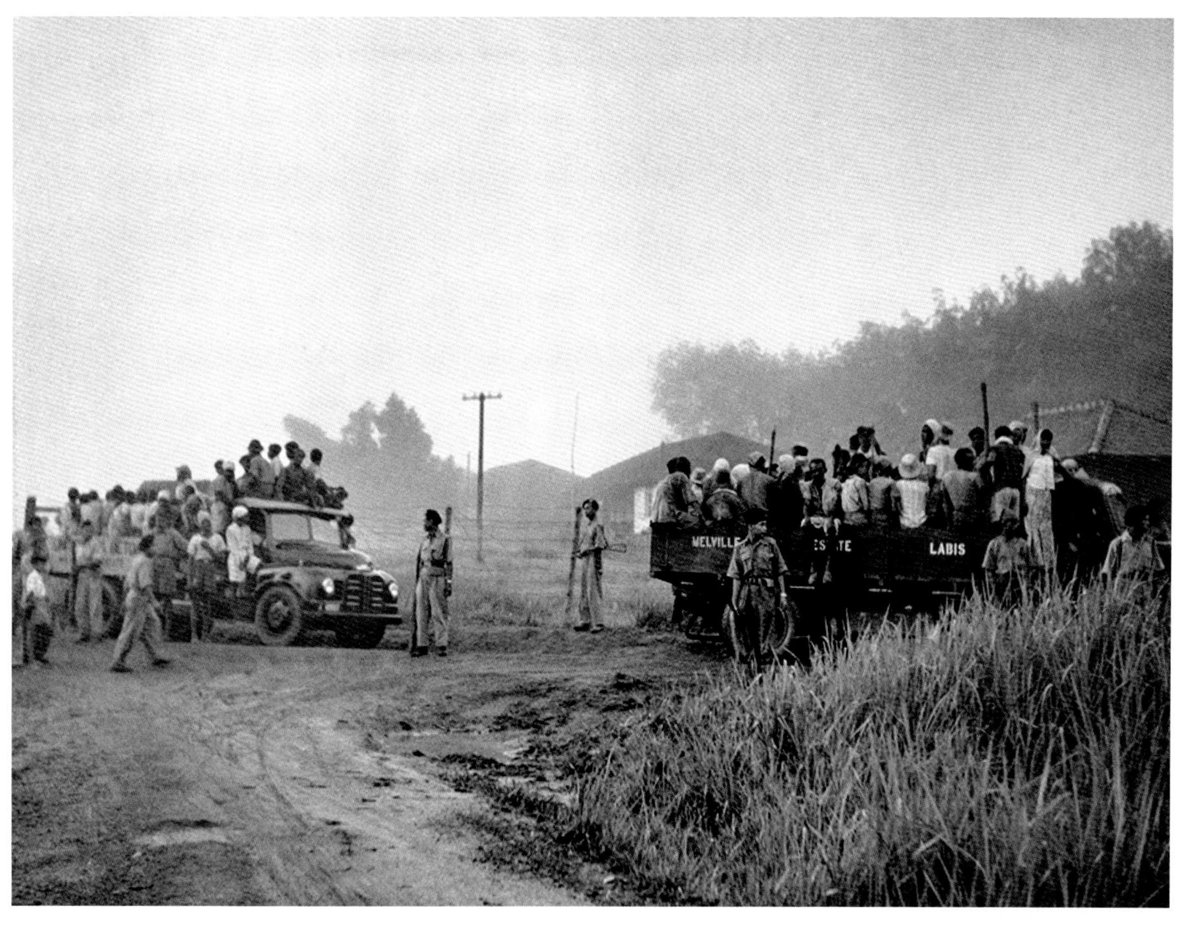

Attacks by the MNLA on the two vital industries – rubber and tin production – pushed the colonial authorities into increasing security around plantations, mines and factories. The workers at these sites were especially vulnerable to attack or pressure from the communist forces.

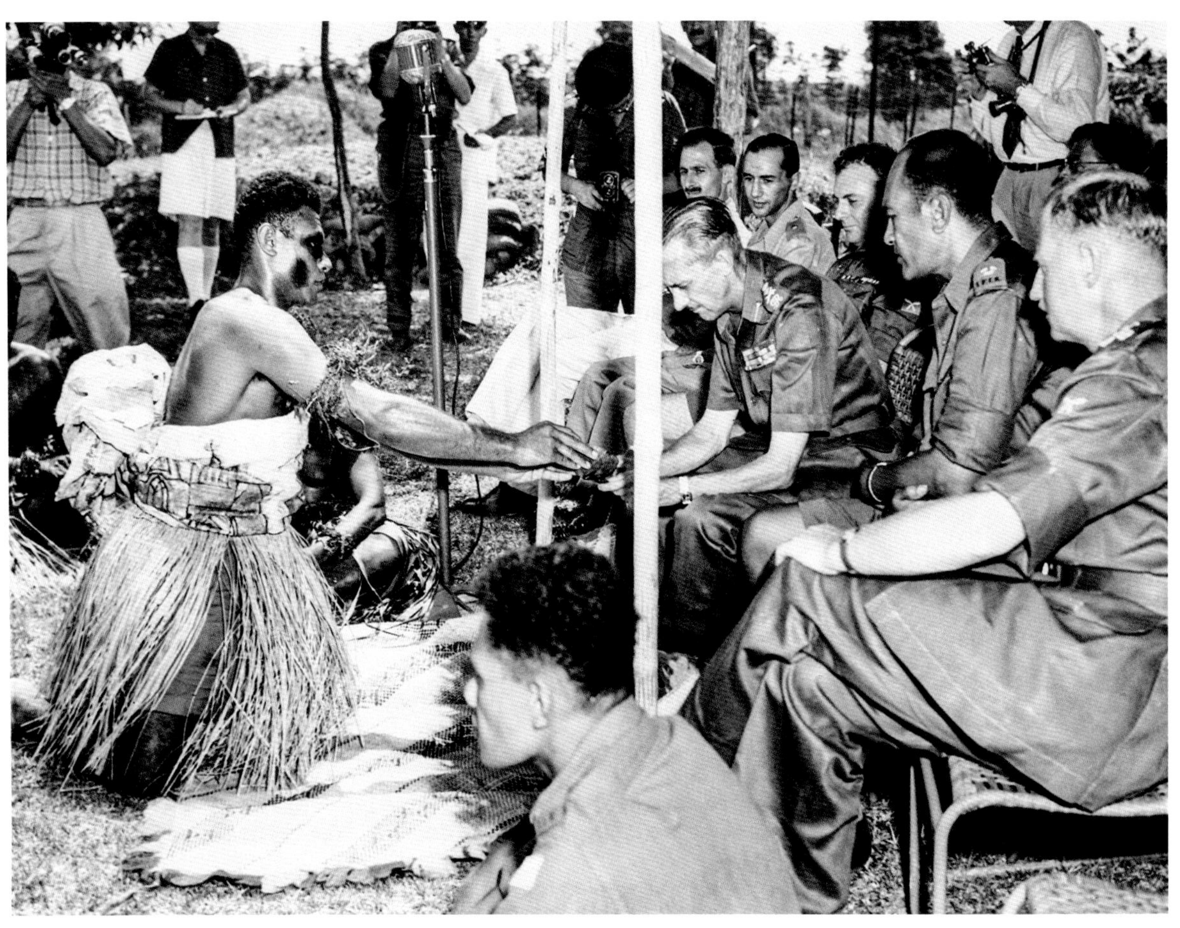

Field Marshal Sir Gerald Templer (centre) became High Commissioner of Malaya in 1952. His 'hearts and minds' approach to running the conflict in Malaya combined welfare improvements with harsh control. He built roads, clinics and schools, but also oversaw mass deportations, food restrictions and forced resettlement. His policies were designed to gain support from civilians, while simultaneously weakening the insurgency.

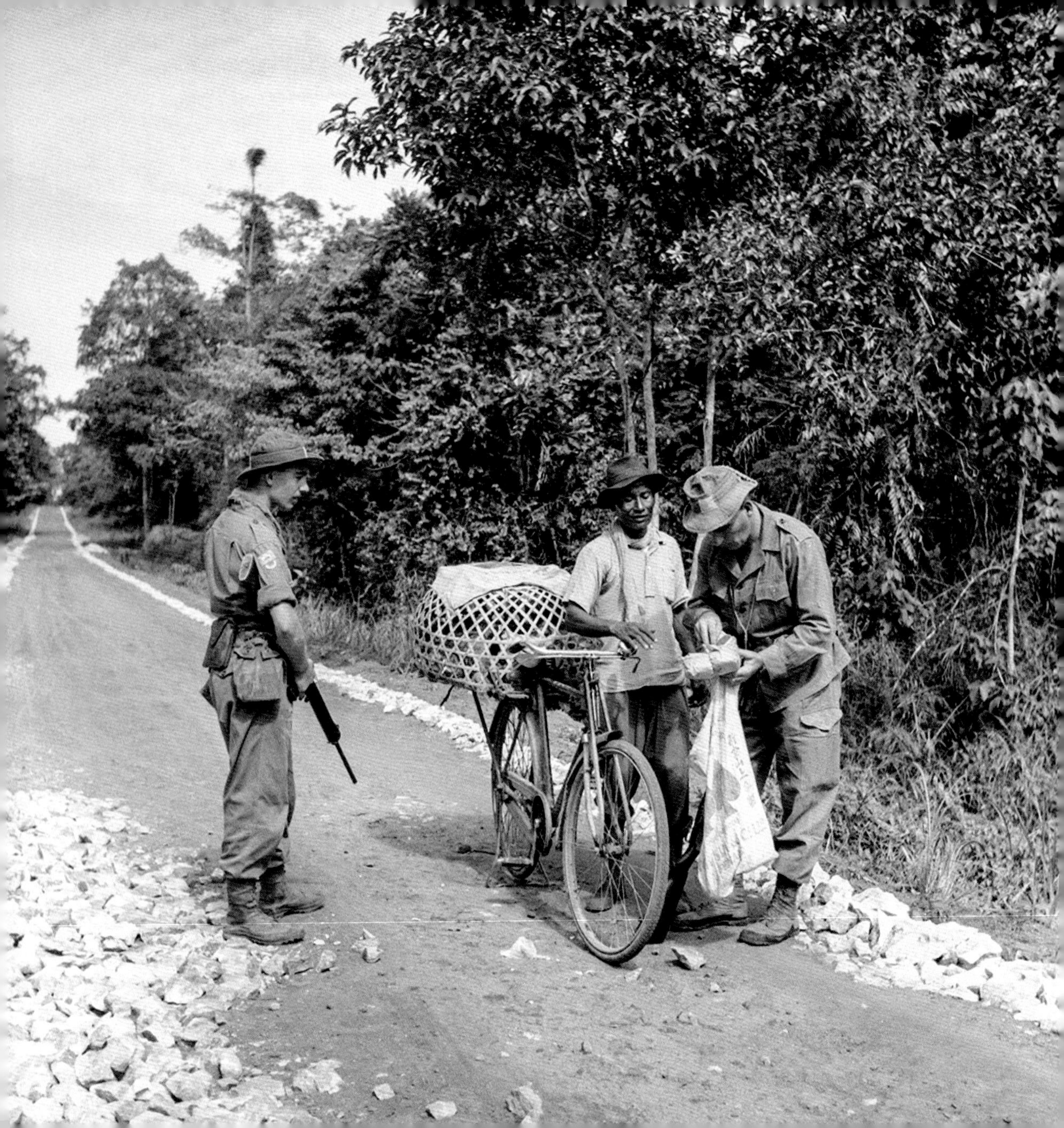

British tactics combined fighting insurgents in the jungle with separating the MNLA from its local support. To do this, the colonial authorities implemented the 'Briggs Plan', which forcibly resettled around half a million people into guarded 'New Villages'. They hoped to starve the insurgents of food and medicine, and prevent them attracting new members and followers. People were searched as they entered and departed the villages to ensure they were not passing supplies to the MNLA.

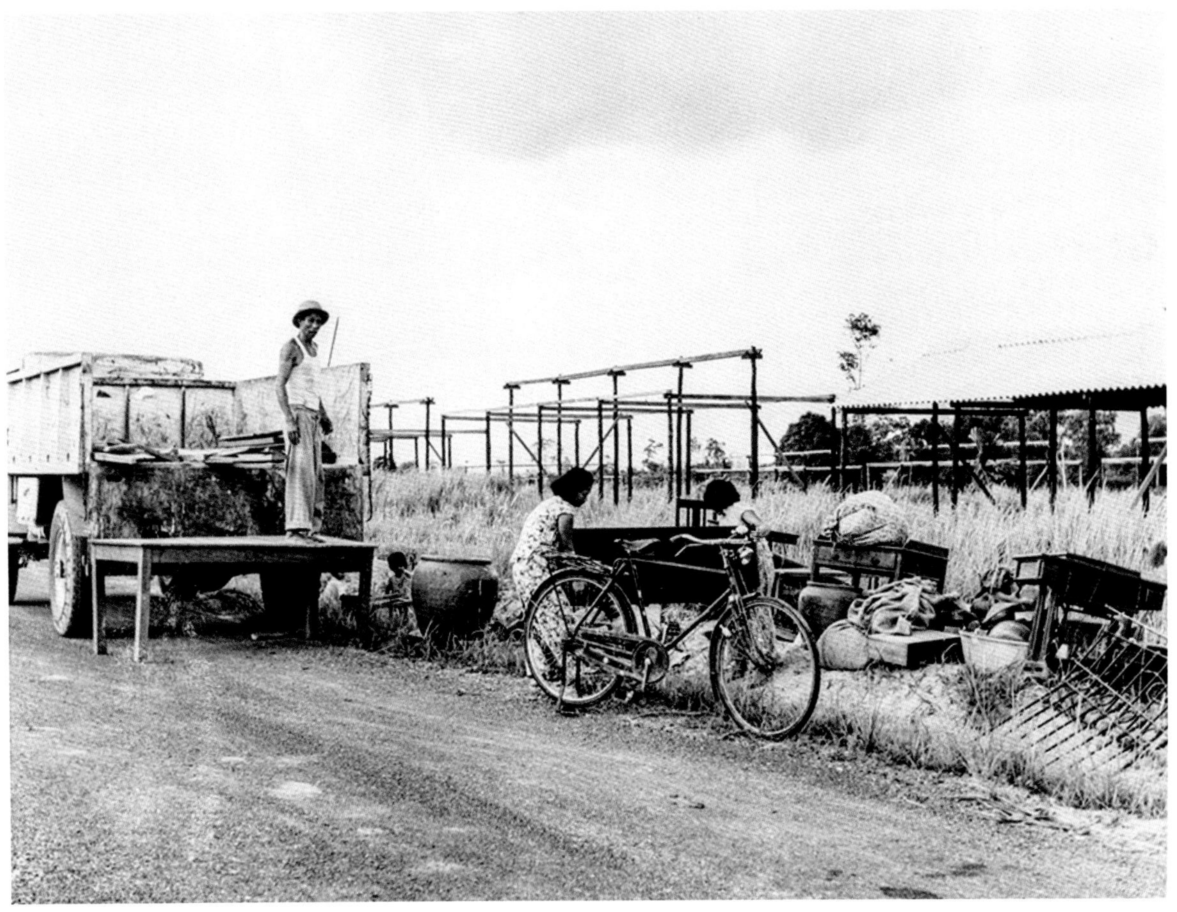

The New Villages were in fact guarded settlements with barbed wire fences, into which the rural population, mainly ethnic Chinese, were resettled. They had previously lived independently on land close to the edge of the jungle, in groups with strong social and family ties. When they arrived at the New Villages, they had to start again from scratch – building new homes and lives. The colonial authorities controlled where they could go, when they could leave and even what, when and how much they ate.

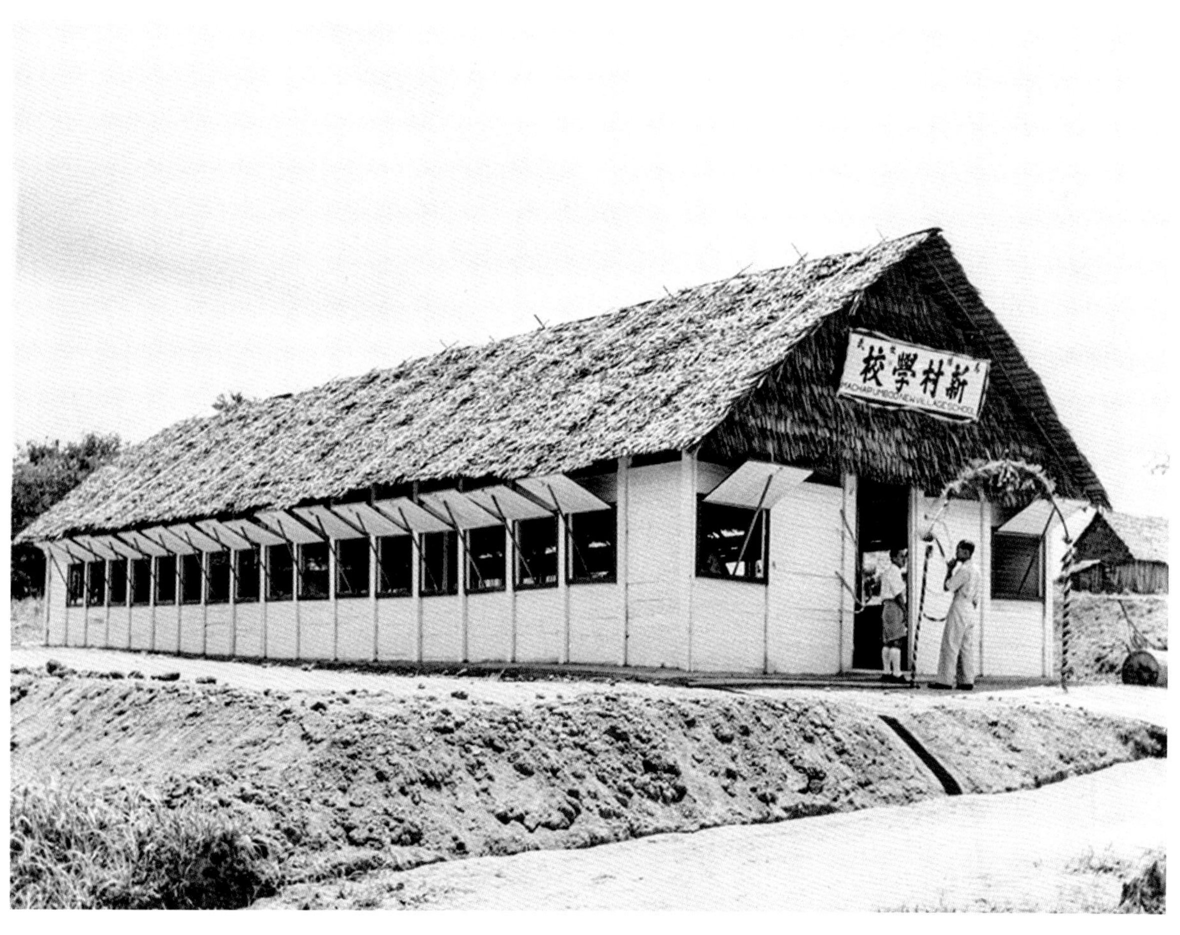

A newly built school in a New Village. Some villages were entirely new, while others were adapted from existing settlements. Most followed a standard layout: rows of houses, a market, police post and basic public and community buildings. Watchtowers and barbed wire fencing controlled where people could enter and leave.

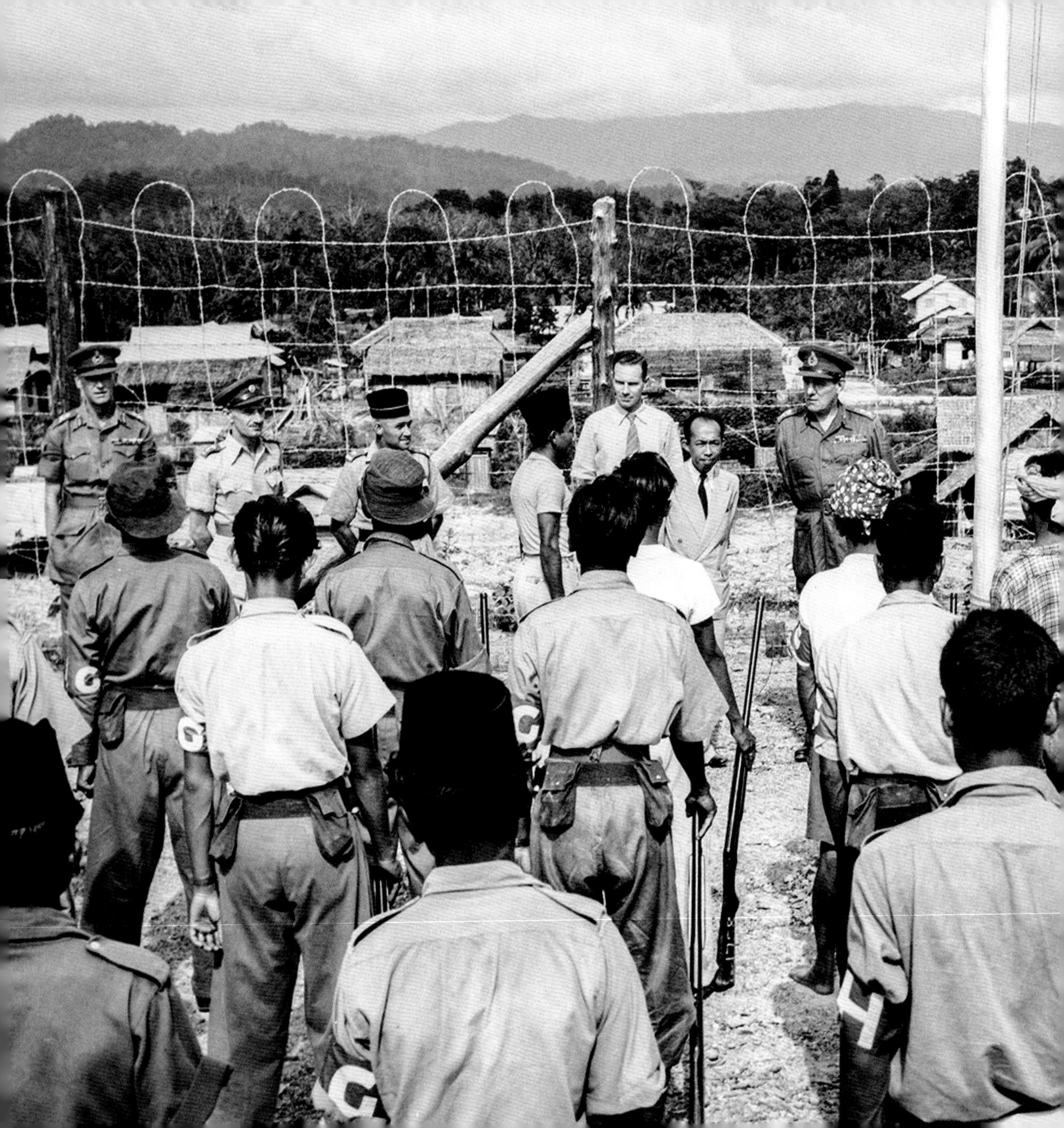

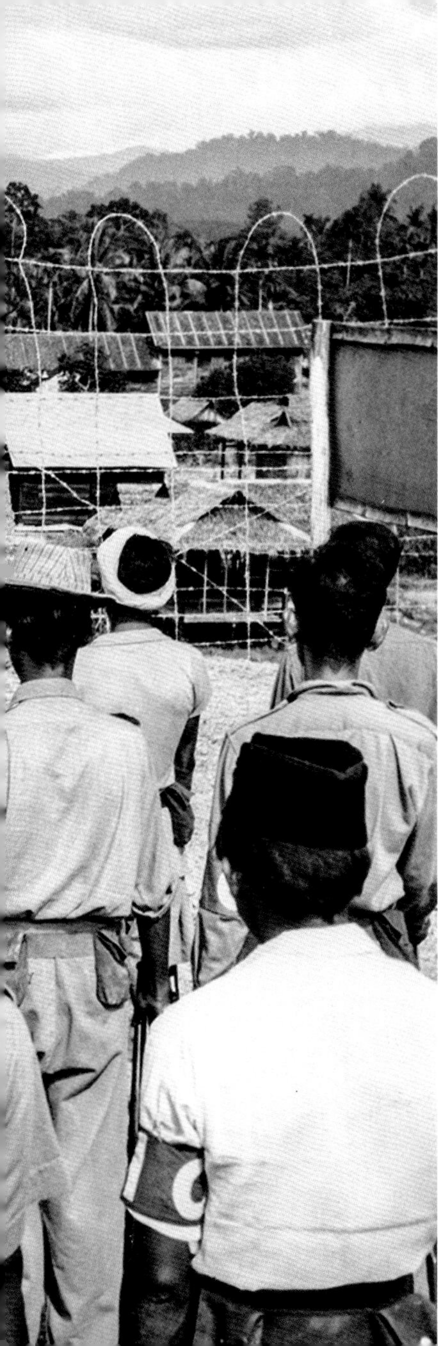

Lieutenant General Sir Geoffrey Bourne addresses Home Guard recruits. Service in the Home Guard was unpaid and voluntary. Duties included patrolling the village and supporting the army and police. Many were armed. These locally-raised defence forces became a key part of the colonial campaign, but also represented deepening social and ethnic divisions within Malaya.

British soldiers take a break mid-patrol. Routine, fatigue and discomfort shaped the day-to-day experience of jungle warfare. British soldiers were often accompanied by members of locally raised forces, known as Civil Liaison Officers. They served as guides and interpreters for the British troops.

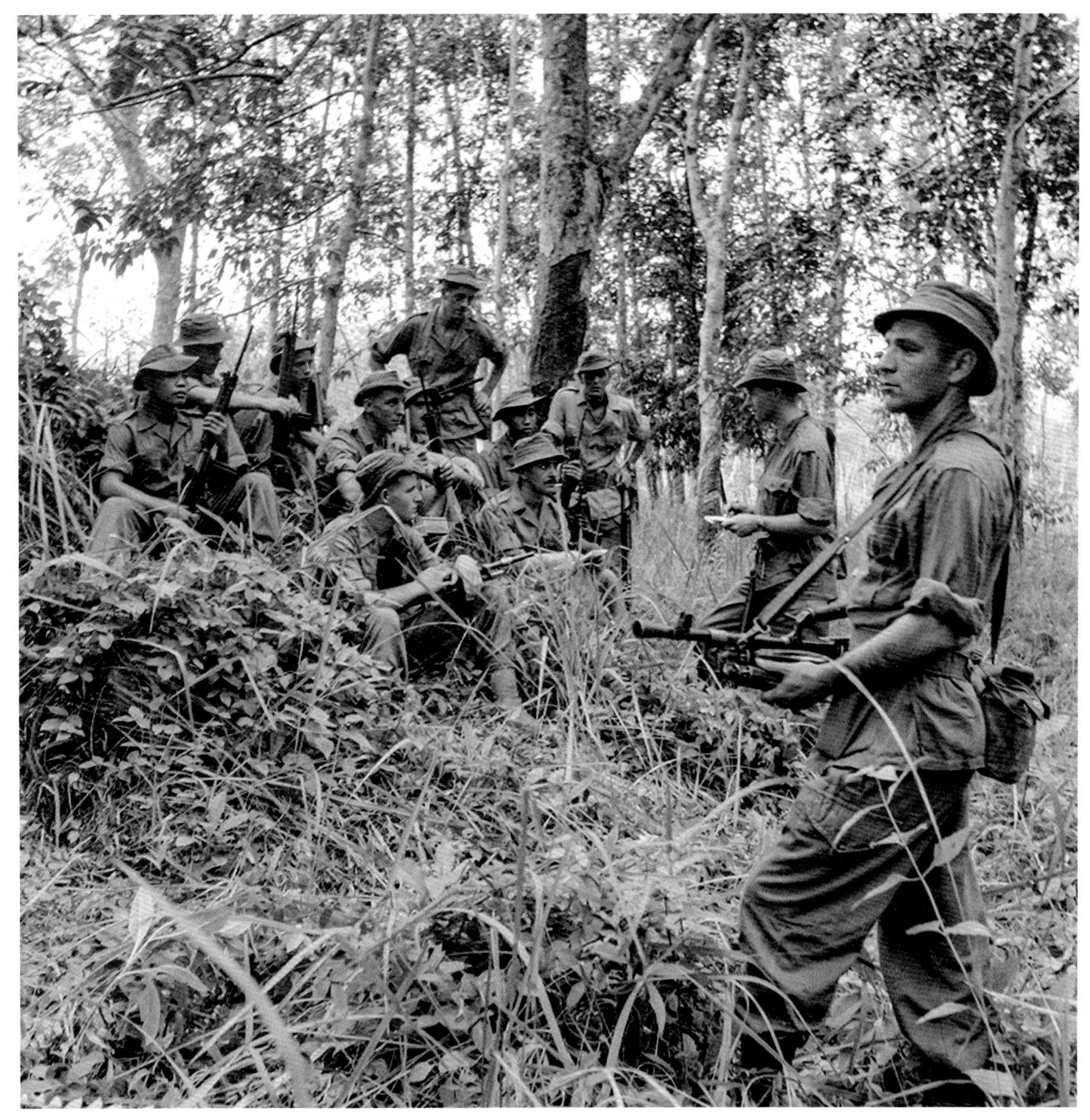

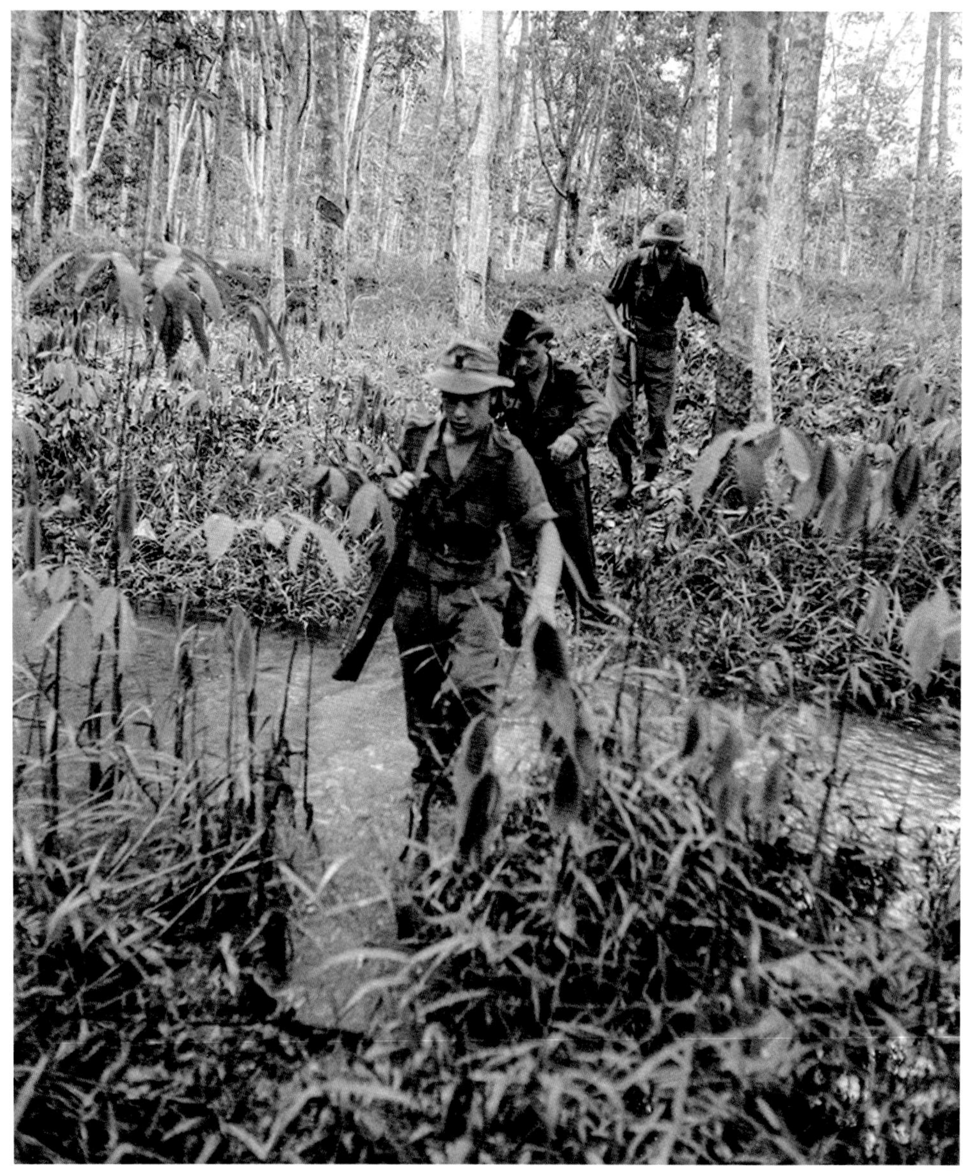

British soldiers move cautiously through water in the Malayan jungle. Many were National Servicemen, conscripted to serve in the military for two years. One Suffolk Regiment soldier recalled: 'Some terrain was worse...in particular the swamps...It is very, very eerie to be waist high in murky, swampy water, not knowing really what your next foot is going to do. It saps the strength.'

Members of 22 SAS Regiment between operations. Highly-trained and lightly-equipped, their role in Malaya was to work with local and regular forces. They patrolled deep into the jungle, often for extended periods of several weeks and were supplied by air. Specific patrol aims varied, with one overriding objective: to kill large numbers of so-called 'CTs', (Communist Terrorists).

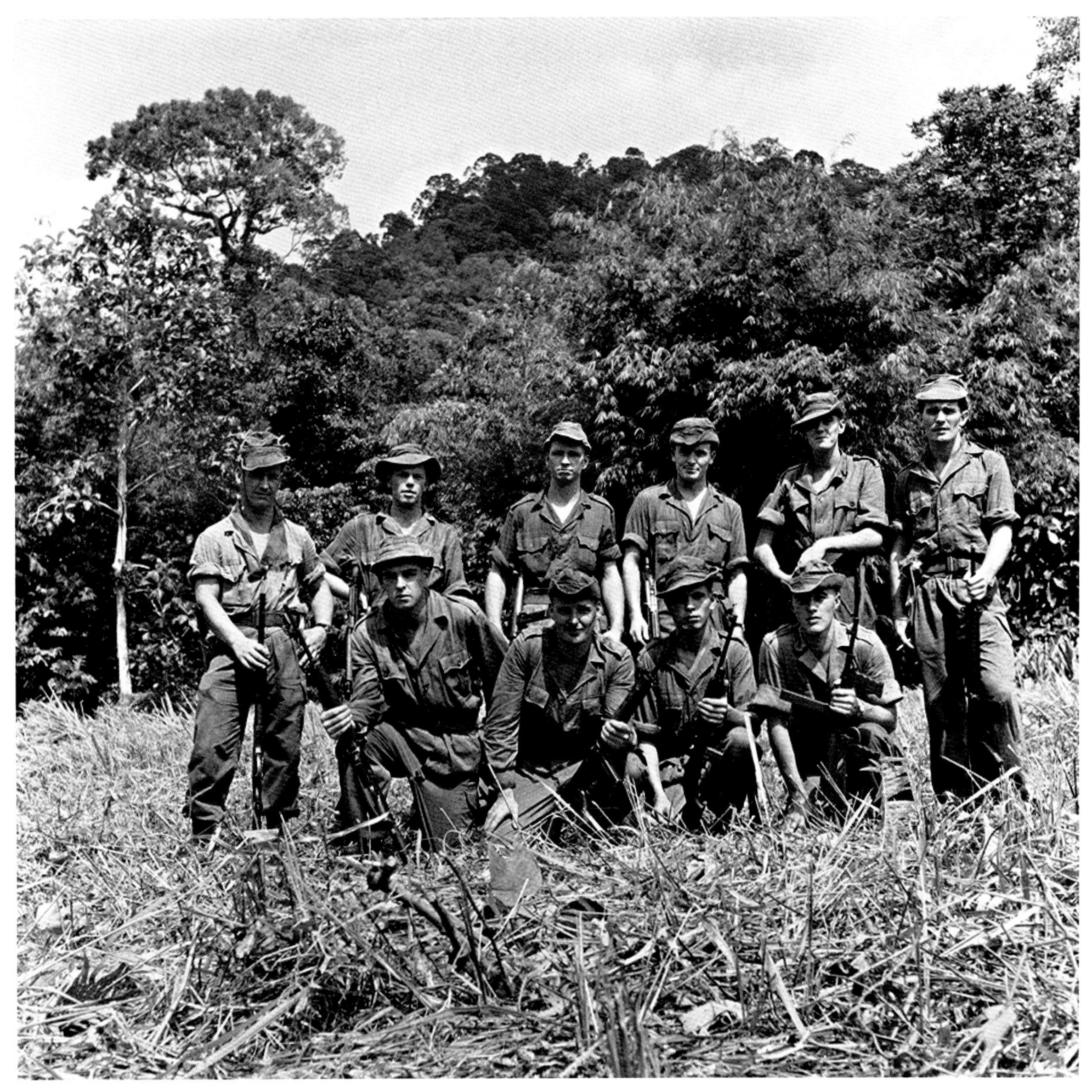

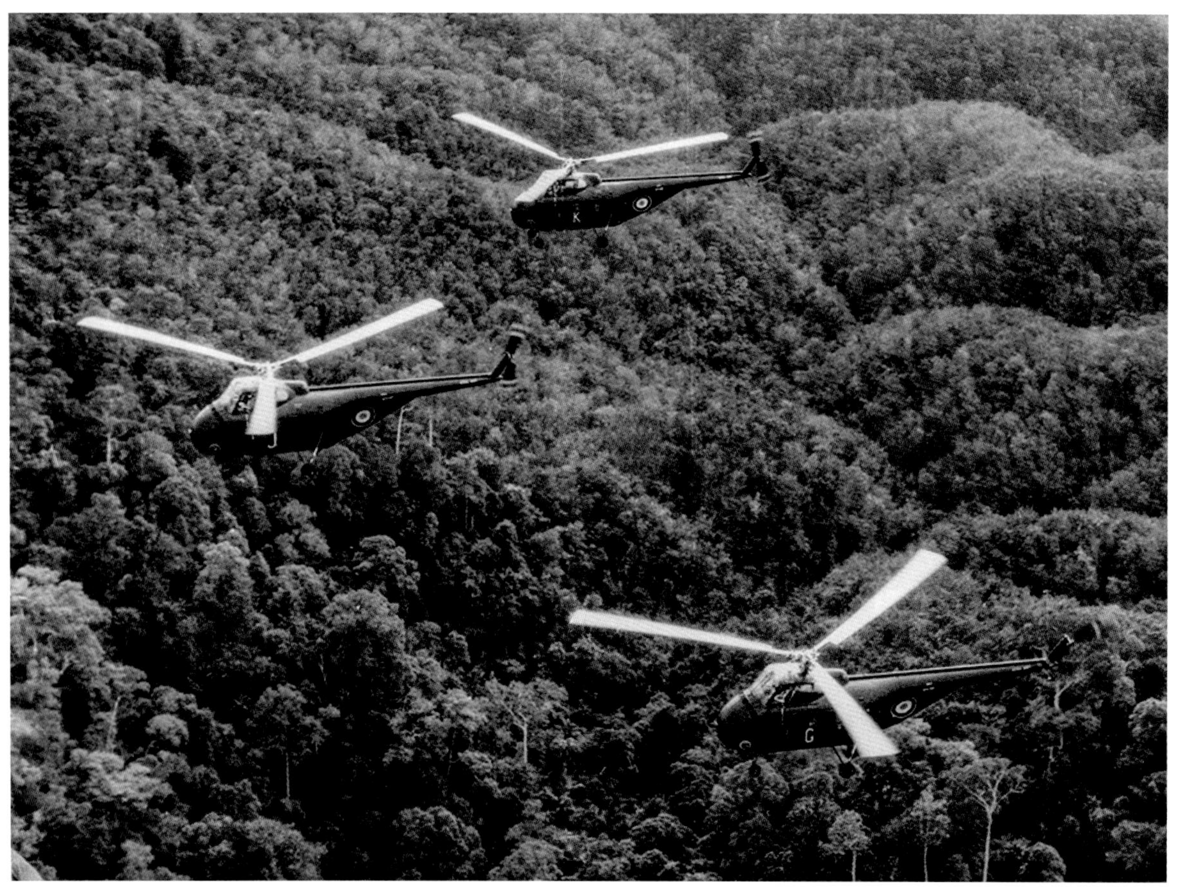

Royal Navy Sikorsky helicopters of No. 848 Naval Air Squadron fly over the jungle canopy. Air support provided faster movement of troops and supplies. While air support alone could not secure control, it played a crucial role is making remote areas more accessible, especially during long campaigns deep in the jungle.

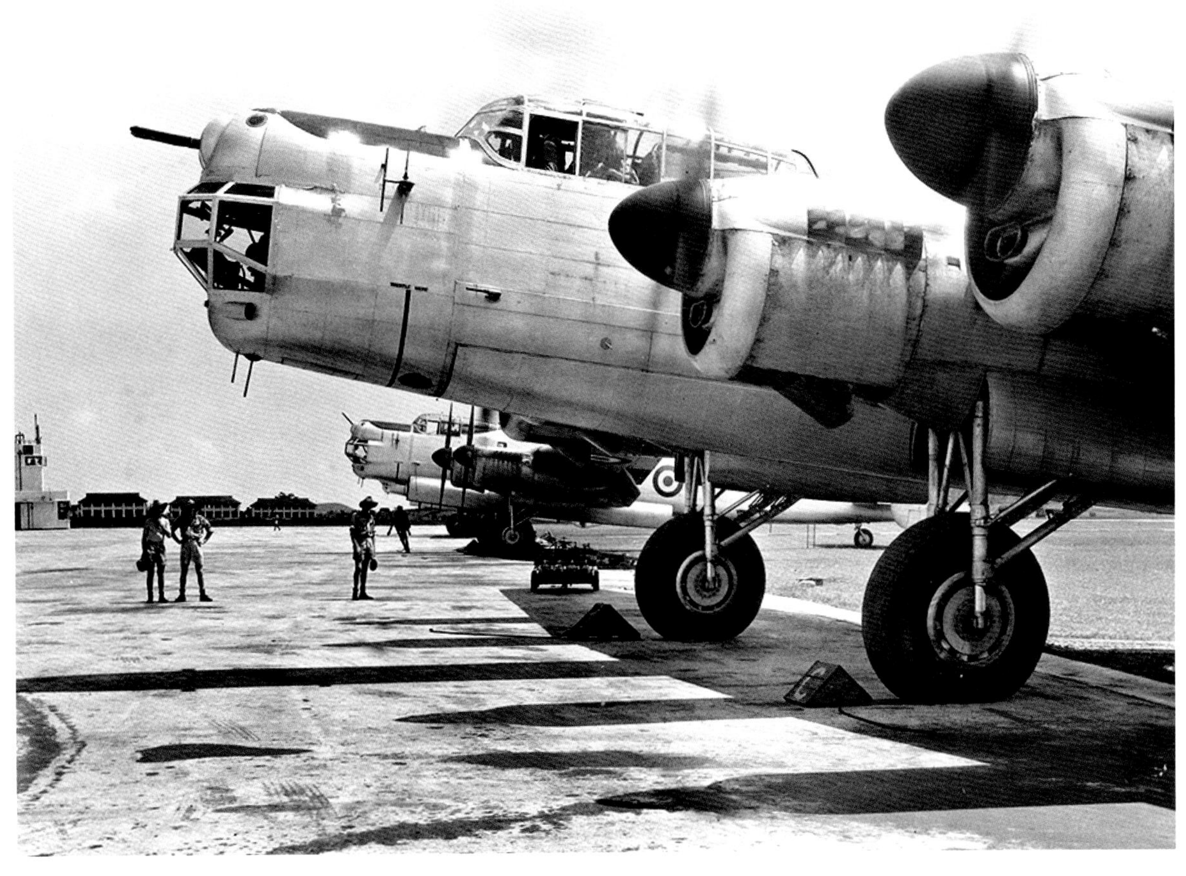

Australian bombers are armed before a jungle sortie. Although lacking precision, bombing raids on jungle areas were designed to disrupt MNLA forces.

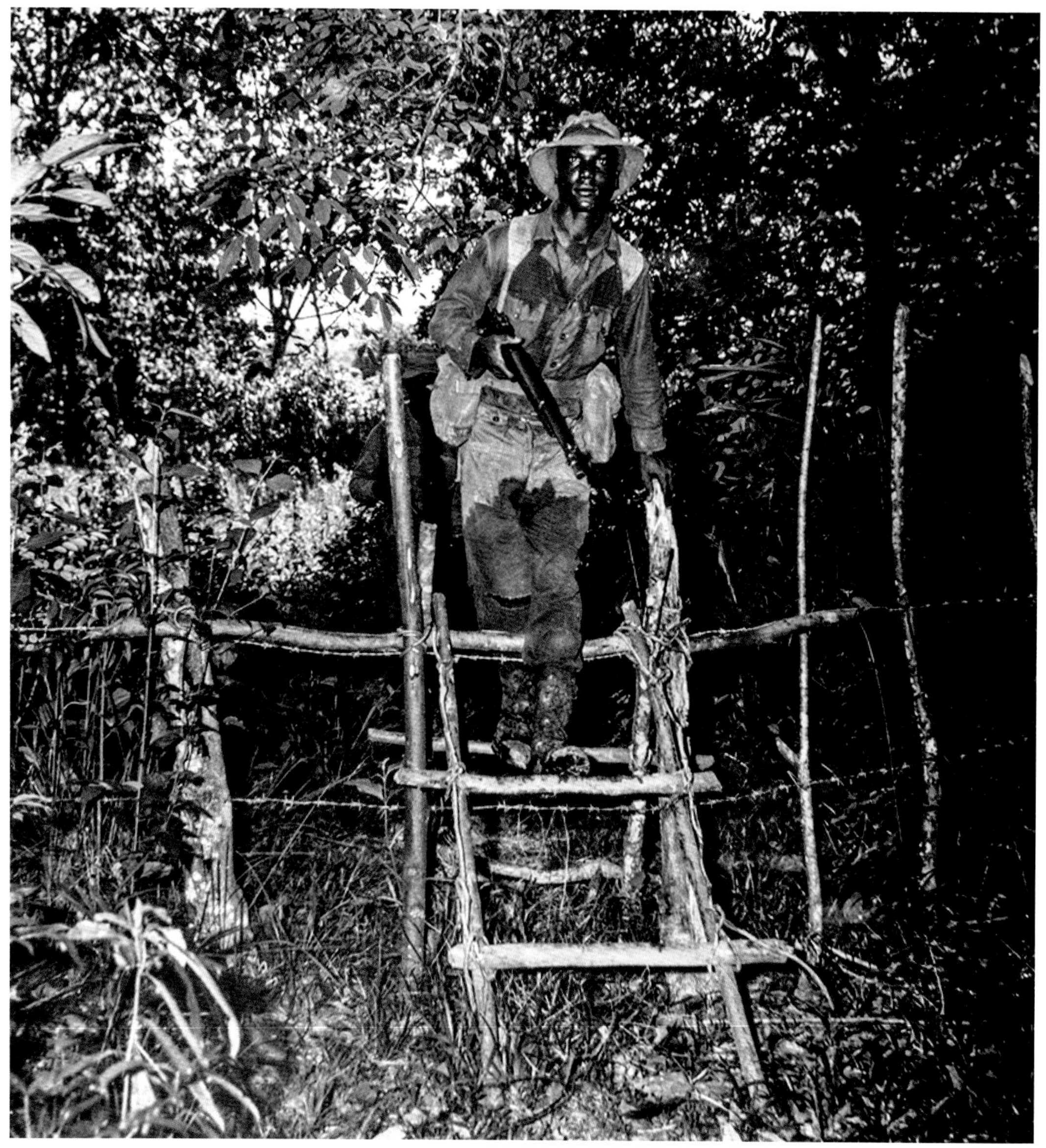

A Kenyan soldier from the King's African Rifles on a jungle patrol in Malaya. The colonial authorities relied on troops from other parts of the Commonwealth. Some served in two or three of the 'emergencies'. Their presence shows how Britain managed multiple conflicts with a mix of imperial and local manpower.

Communist attacks and British tactics hit civilians hardest. The MNLA and colonial forces heavily disrupted the lives of the people of Malaya. Ethnic Chinese communities, in particular, were targeted by both sides. For many, the 'emergency' was not a war of ideology but a daily struggle to survive amid violence, suspicion and pressure from all directions. Here, Malayan civilians are photographed by a British soldier, in front of buildings destroyed by the MNLA.

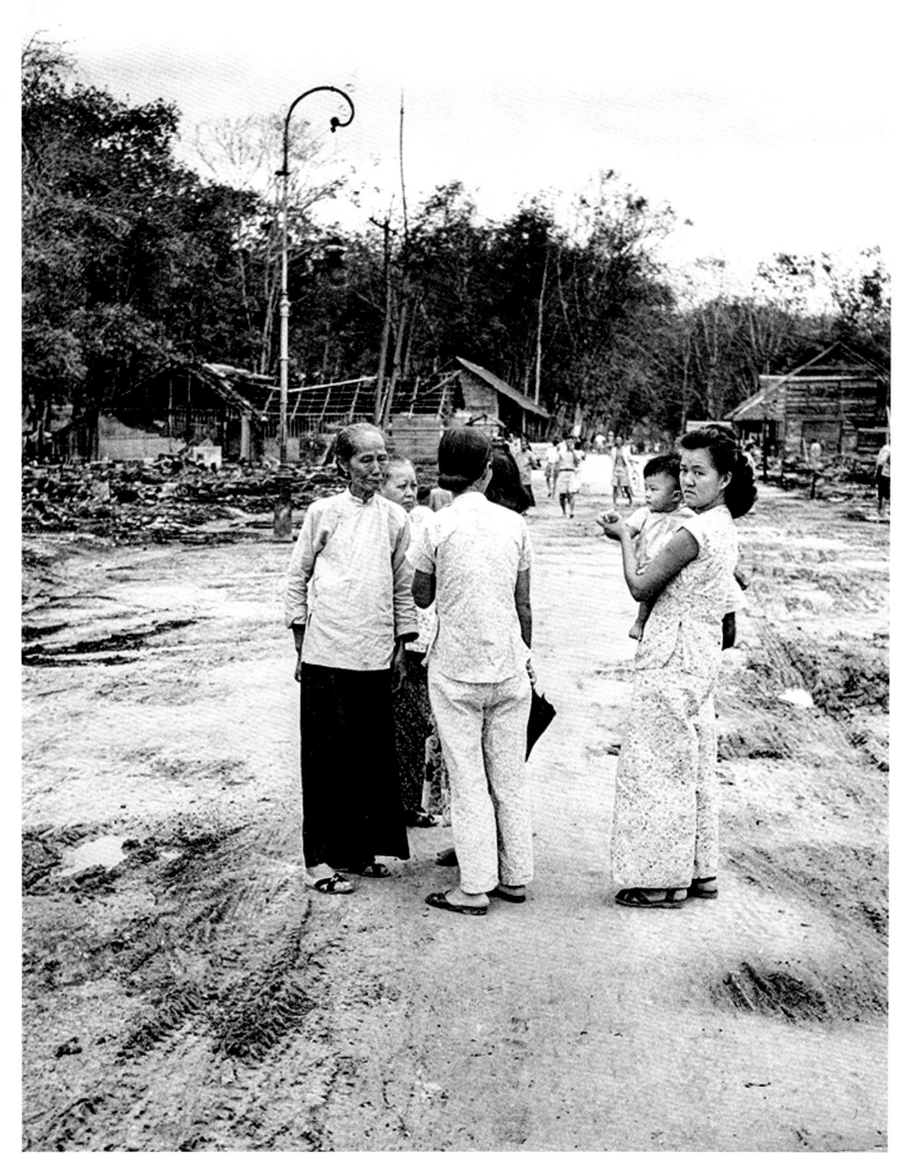

Born in 1936, one of ten siblings, Yong Ching Huat and his family were resettled from a nearby area to Yong Peng New Village, Malaya. One day, after having breakfast, he was arrested. 'I was locked up for 28 days and beaten nearly to death...They just took me and asked, "Did you come into contact with the communists?" I kept saying no, but they started beating me. It hurt so much that I couldn't bear it anymore and ended up saying yes. I confessed. Then they locked me up for 28 days. After they let me out, I was called in again after just two nights – for more questioning. All it took was someone saying something and you'd be doomed!'

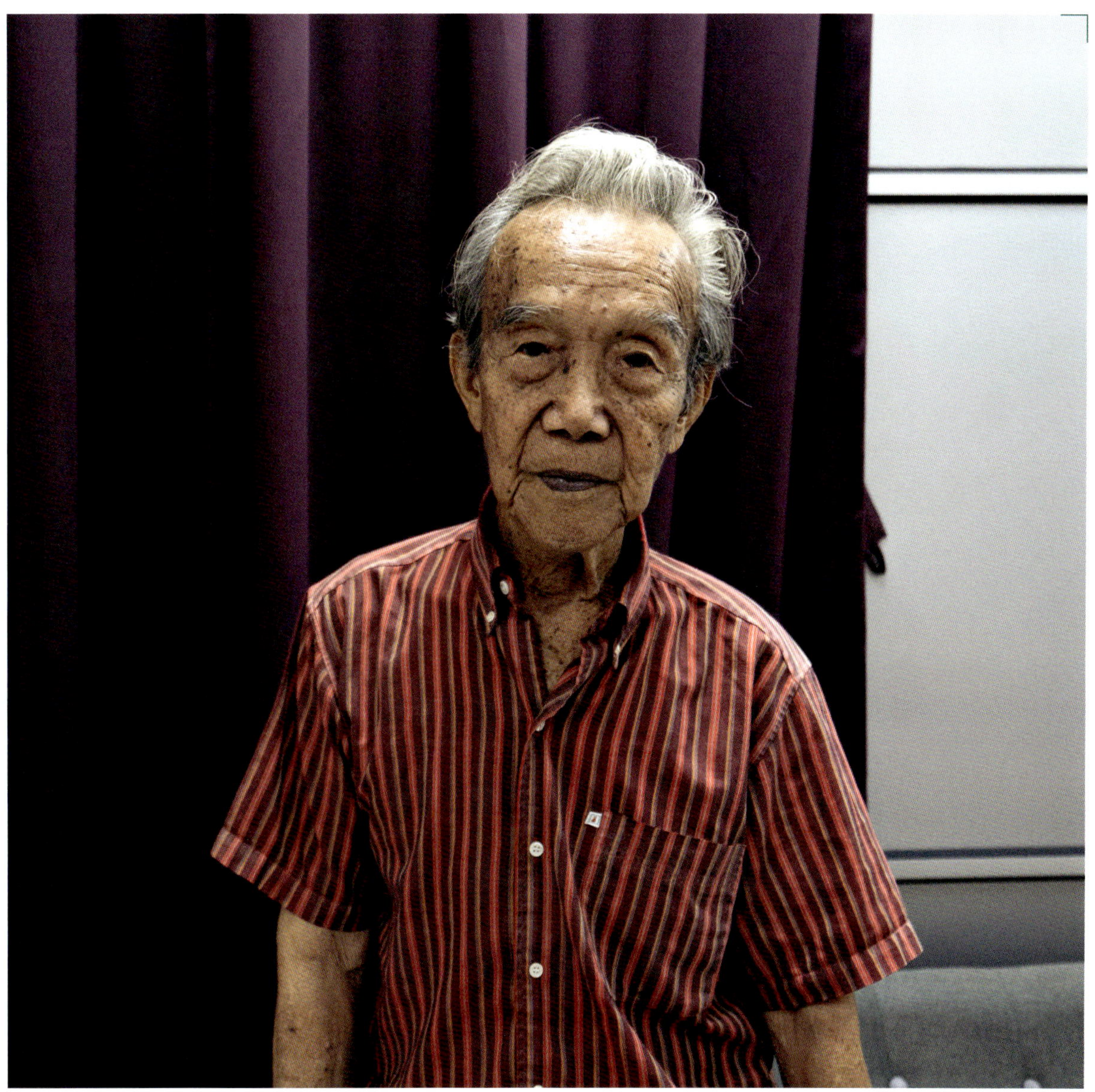

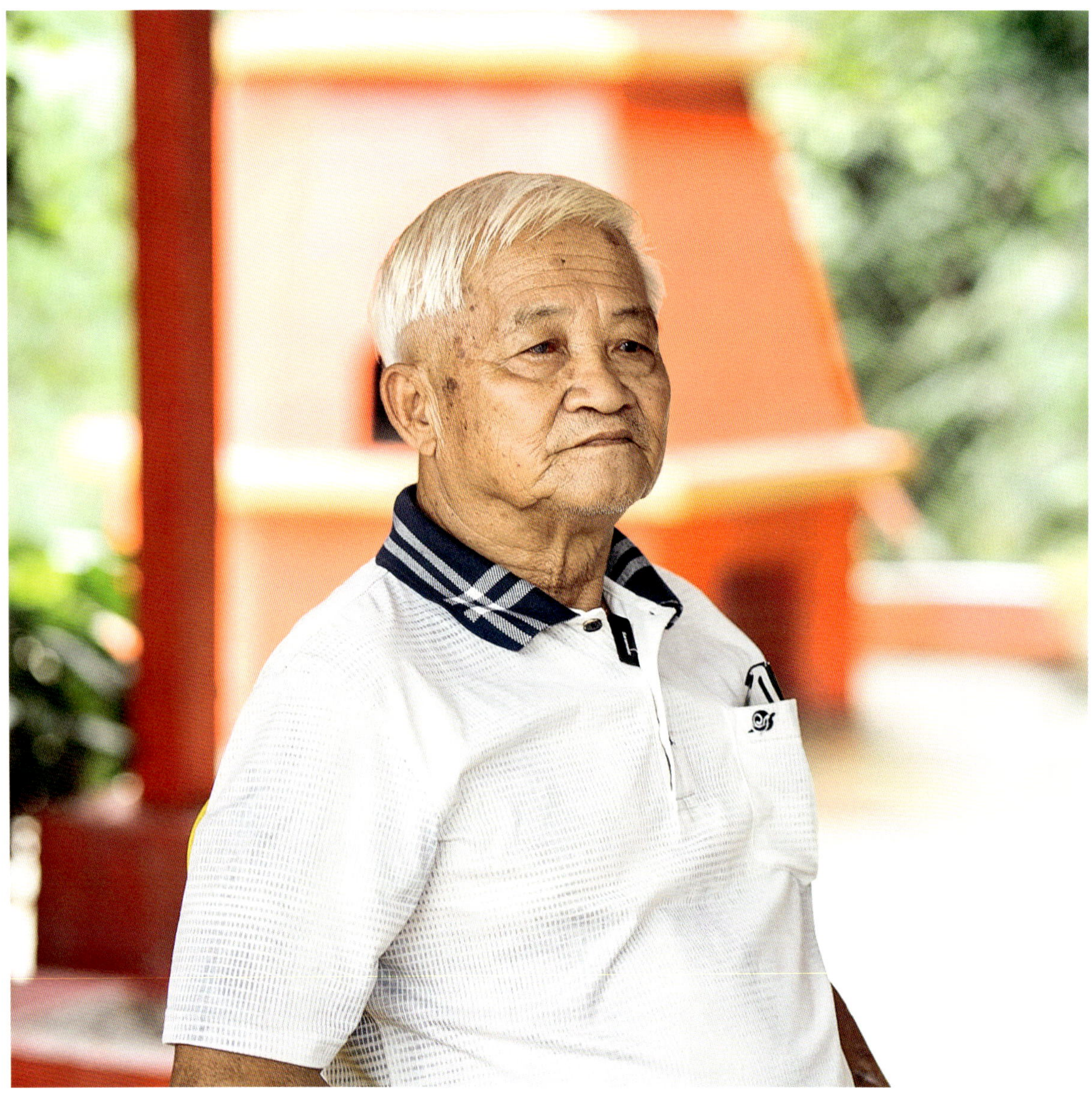

Qin Ah Jin, interviewed in 2024, worked as a rubber tapper in Tras New Village, Malaya. 'It was really hard,' he remembered. 'You were caught between both sides! We were afraid of the government on one side and scared of the communists on the other. That's how it was for people living here back then. I remember my father talking about it. You couldn't offend the communists, and you also couldn't offend the government; wasn't that being caught between a rock and a hard place? Life was really tough back then!'

White settler farms in the fertile central Kenyan highlands were established early in Kenya's colonial history. Their creation pushed tens of thousands of indigenous Kenyans, especially the Kikuyu community, who were barred from owning this lush land, into 'reserves'. At the start of the 'emergency', the farms were targets for Mau Mau attacks. In response, many farms were reinforced with locally-recruited soldiers or police: the one pictured here was turned into a military HQ.

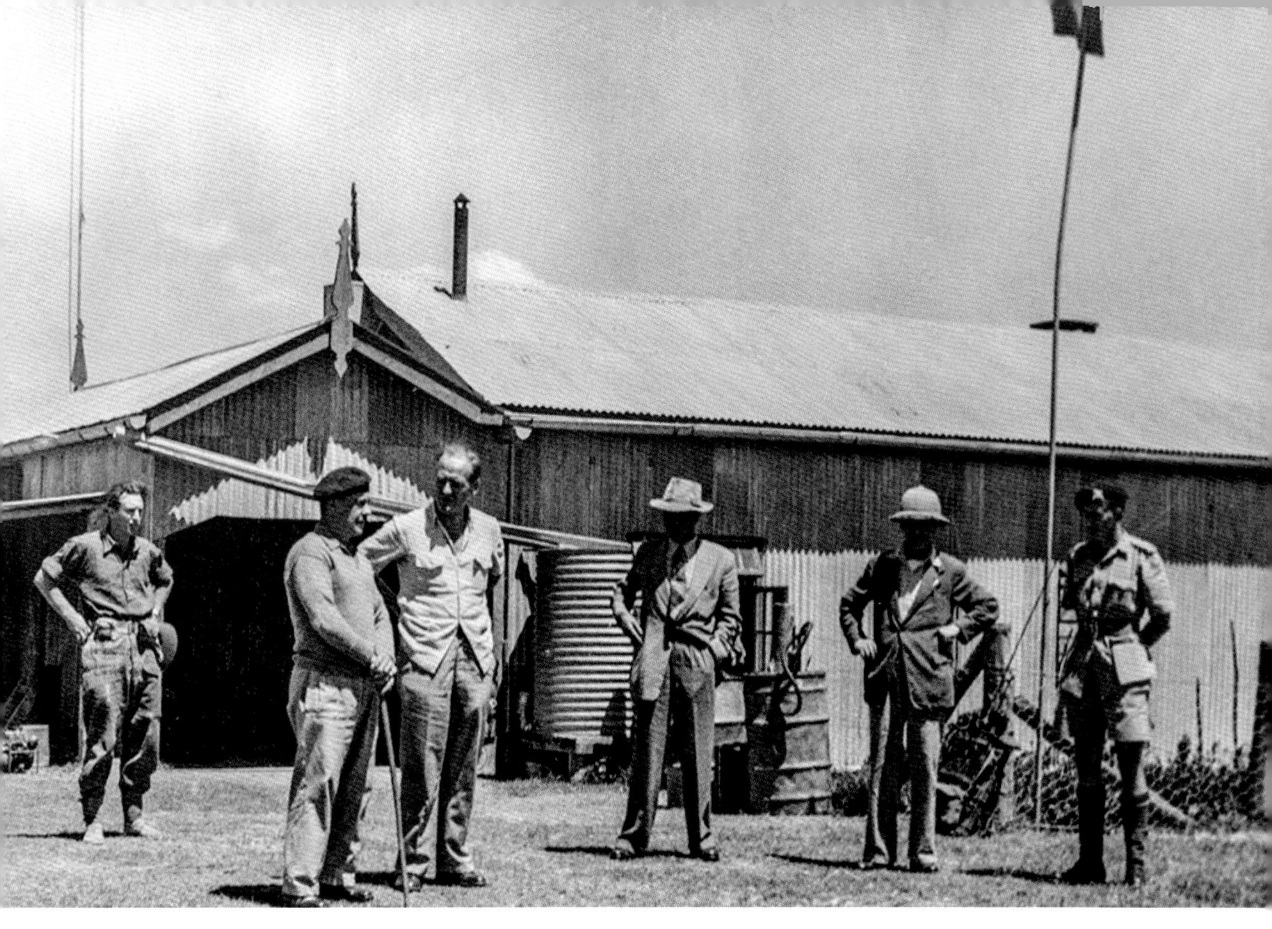

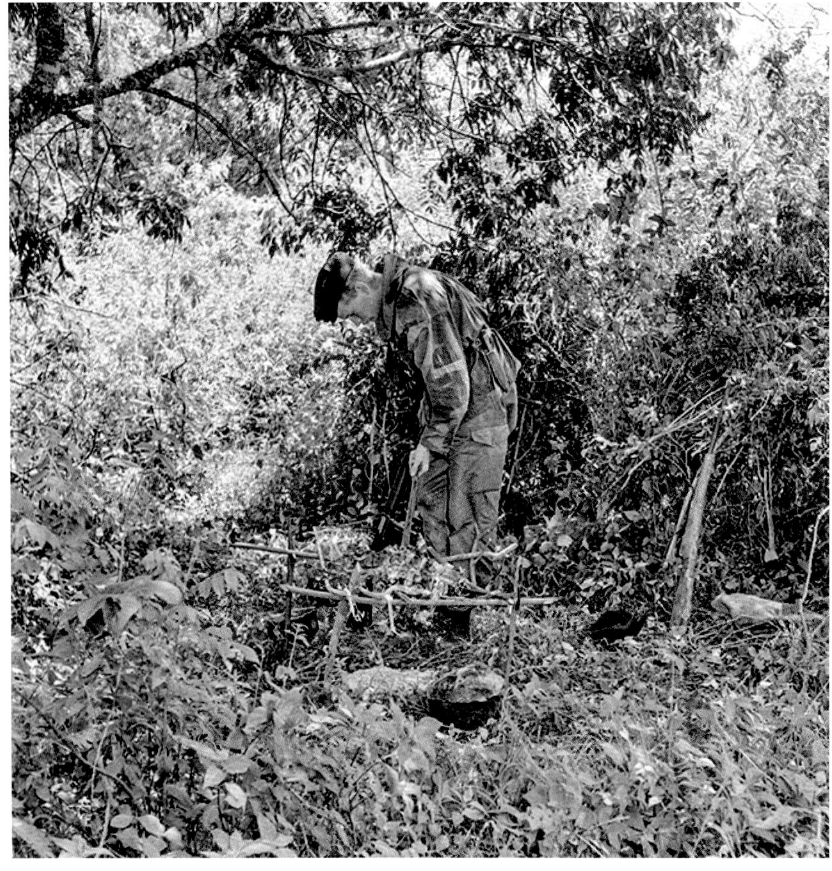

Mau Mau fighters used a mixture of traditional weapons, firearms taken from colonial forces, and homemade weapons such as those shown here. They were made in improvised workshops in the forests, using whatever materials could be gathered, including pipes used for irrigation. The weapons were more often symbolic than practical, aiming to demonstrate that Mau Mau was a credible fighting force.

A British officer inspects an abandoned Mau Mau base. Around 20,000 fighters operated from scattered forest camps, constantly moving to evade British and Kenyan loyalist forces. Mau Mau fighters were depicted by colonial authorities as savage and barbaric. In fact, they debated the future Kenyan state within the forest, and developed elaborate organisational networks to demonstrate their readiness to govern.

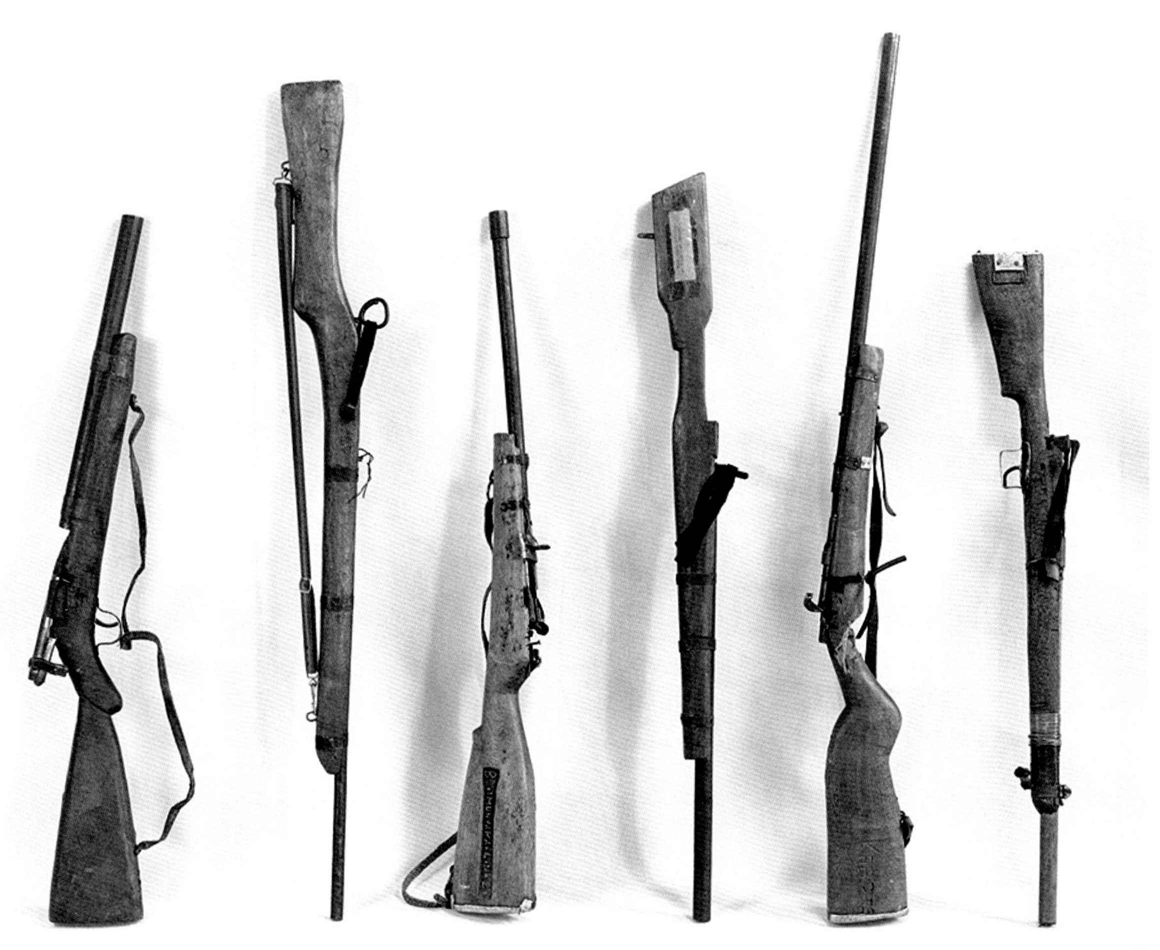

A captured suspected member of Mau Mau is treated by a colonial medic. Although medicine and food were hard for fighters in the forest to obtain, they were sustained by vast support networks, including women and children in nearby villages. Local communities provided food, weapons and intelligence. These supplies were exchanged through intricate secret communication channels, which relied on deep communal trust.

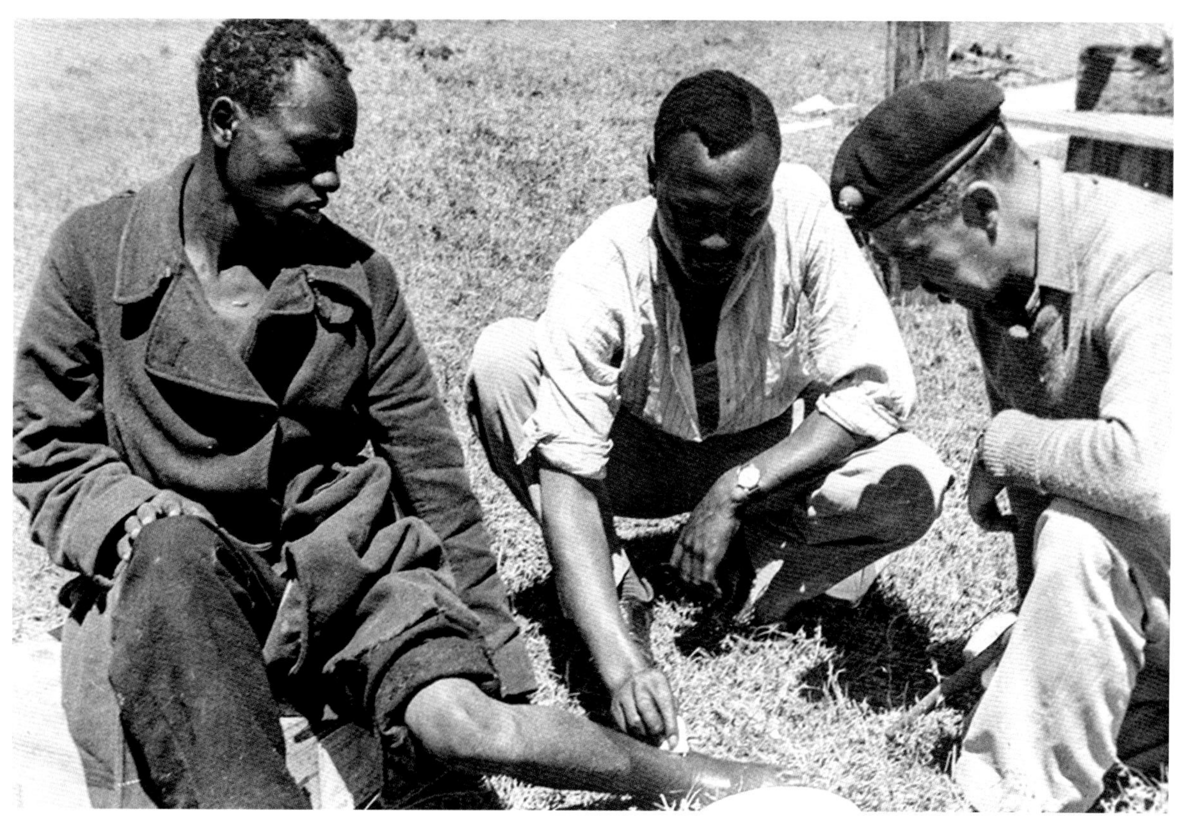

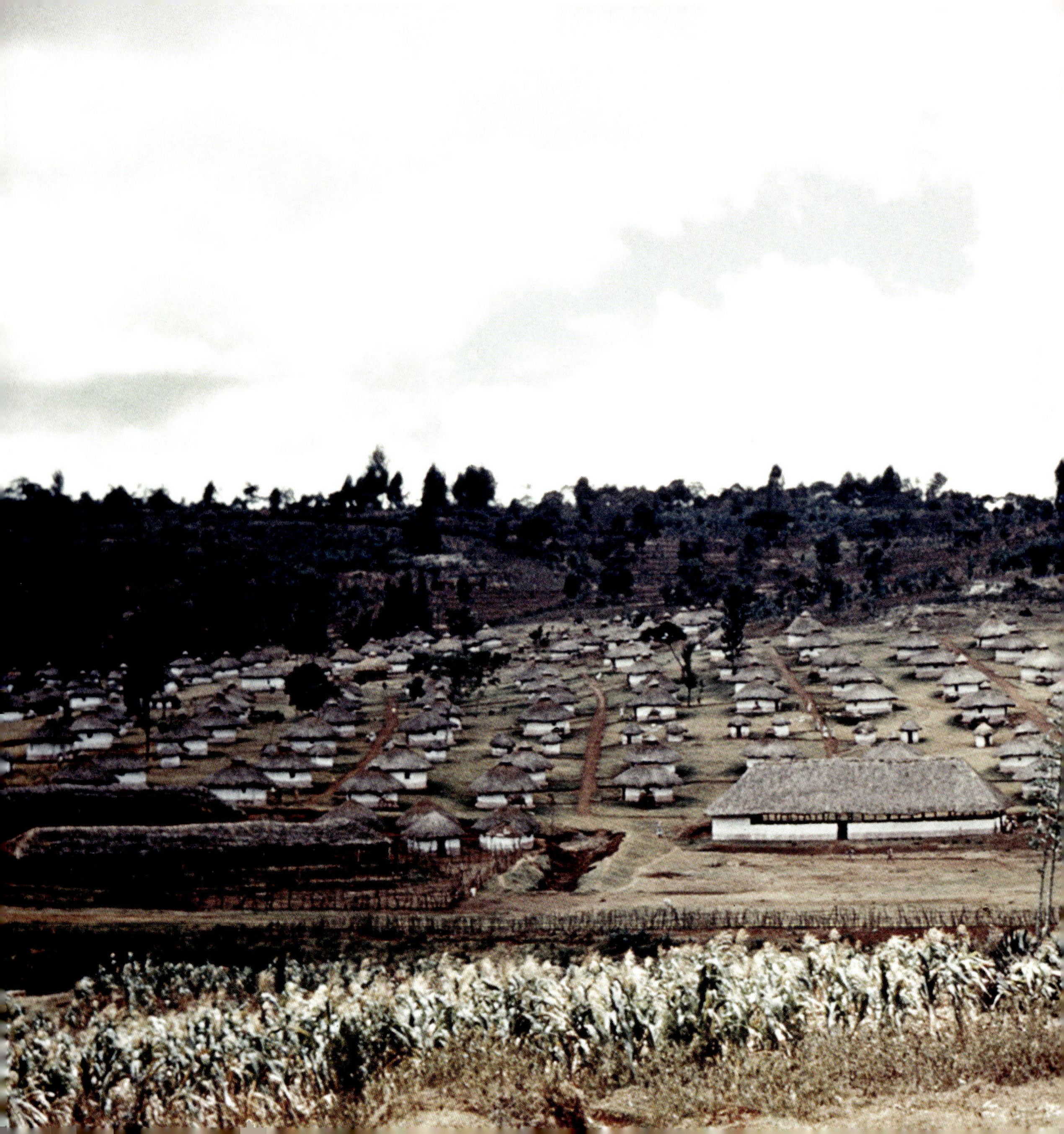

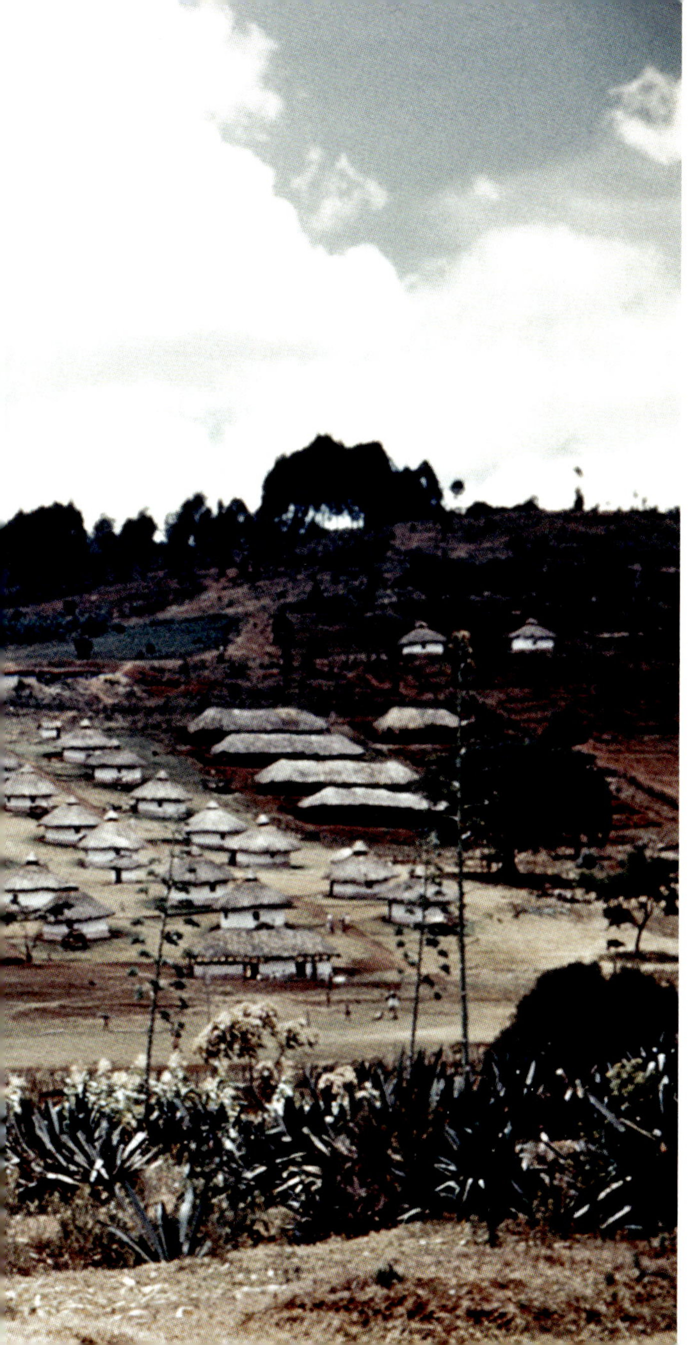

This photograph shows a so-called colonial village – surrounded by trenches and stakes. The villages were built to concentrate the population suspected of maintaining the strongest ties with Mau Mau. Over a million people were forced to move into these villages. There was little privacy, space and no recognition of individual rights. Many people died due to illness, disease, hunger or the harshness of forced labour.

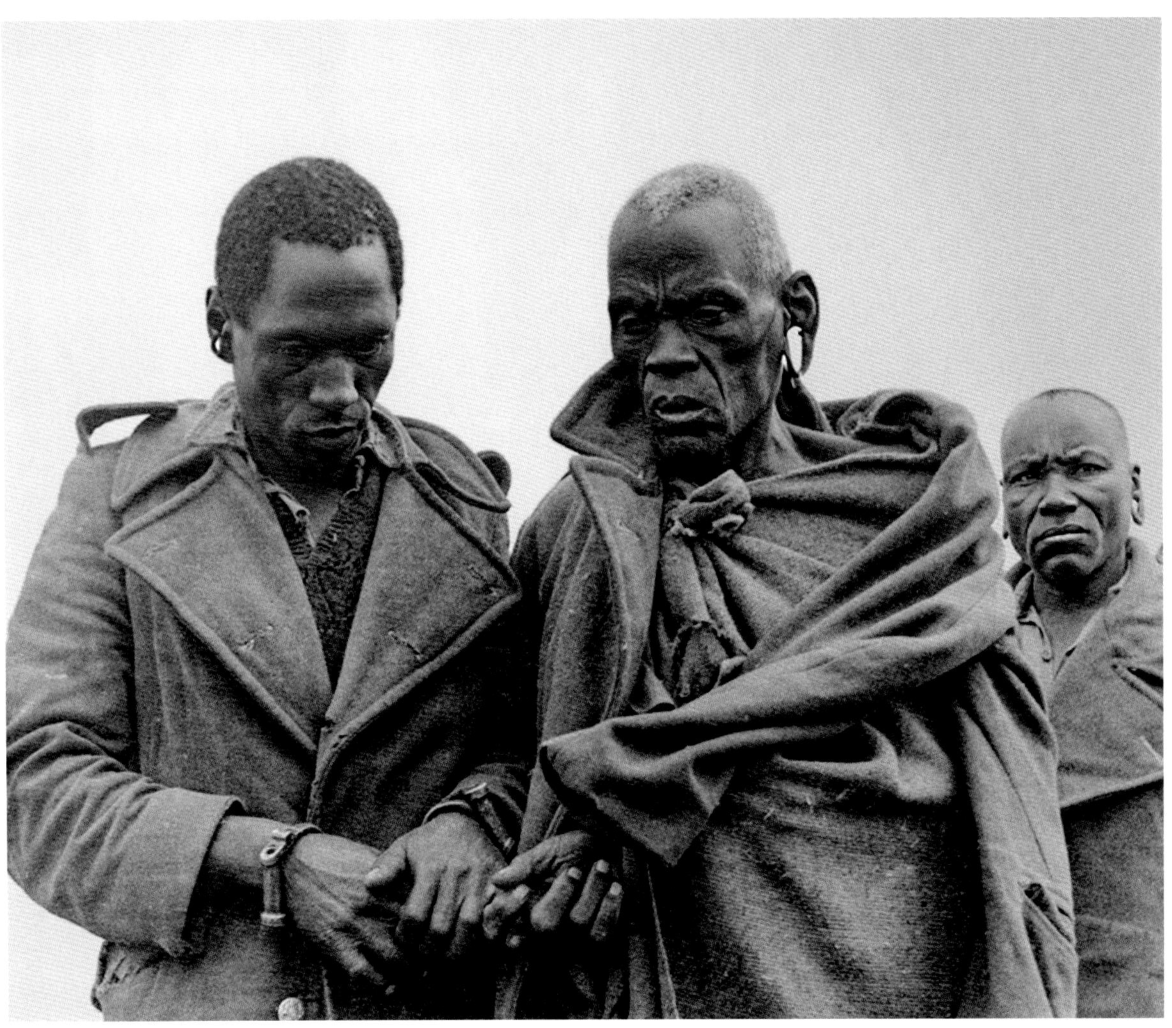

Two Kikuyu men stand under guard. Like many others, they were detained without trial during the 'emergency'. Screening was broad, and guilt was often assumed. Detention became a form of collective punishment.

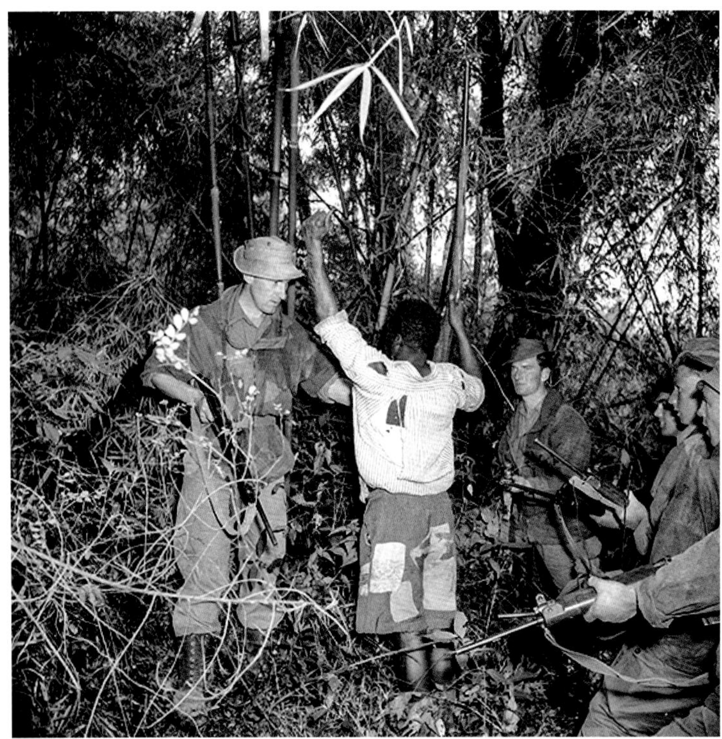

A suspected member of Mau Mau is searched by British troops. In central Kenya, between 1954 and 1956, large numbers of Kikuyu, Embu and Meru people were rounded up and placed in camps. Those that were forcibly relocated to colonial villages could not travel or work without paperwork issued by the colonial authorities. Anyone without a pass would be arrested and detained.

Suspects are questioned before their transfer. Over 80,000 Kenyans were detained without trial in prison camps. Forced labour and torture were used to 'rehabilitate' them away from the ideas promoted by Mau Mau.

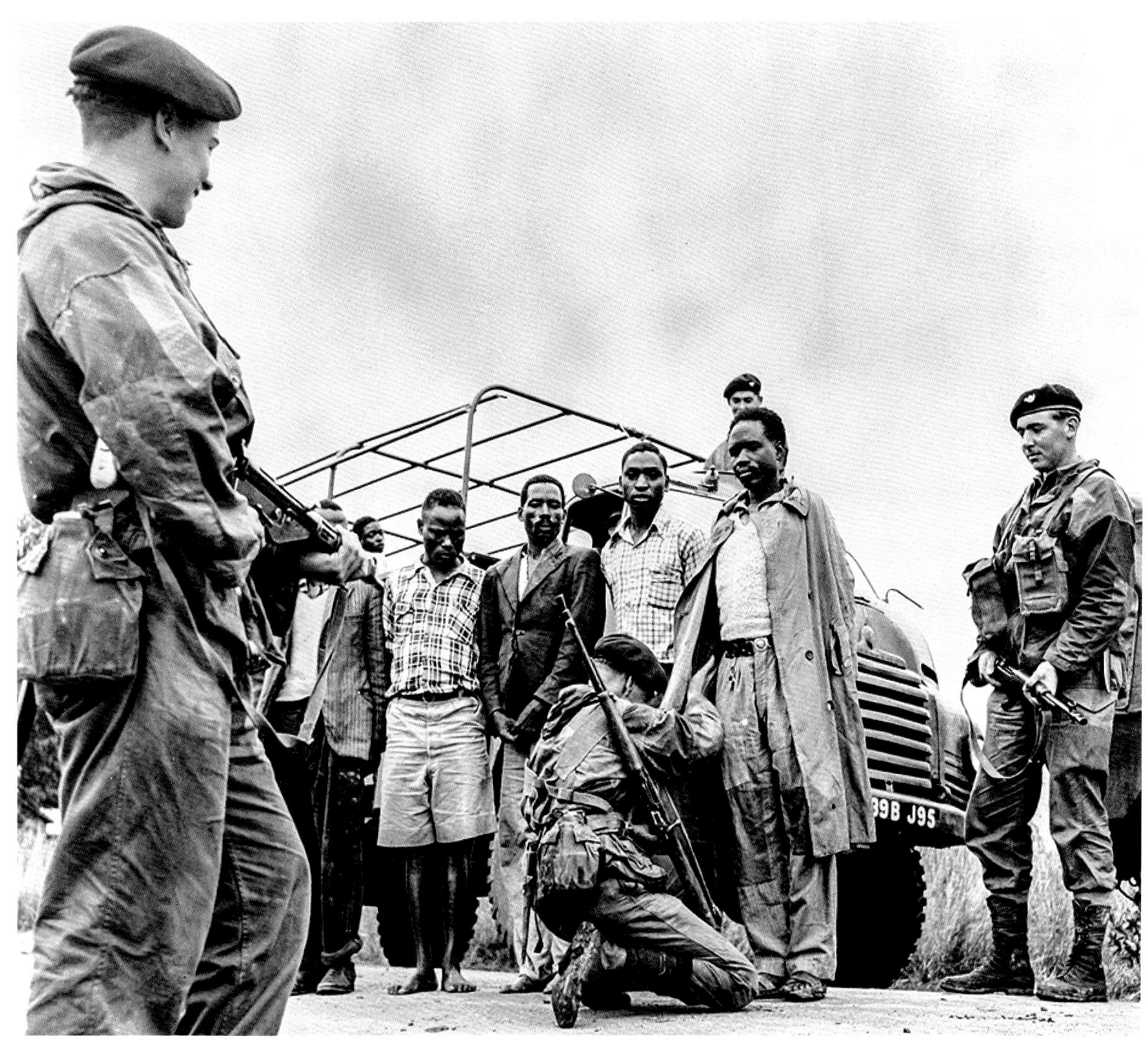
39B J95

Tens of thousands of Kenyan loyalists supported the colonial authorities in the fight against Mau Mau. Their decisions were the result of a complex range of challenges. Some rejected Mau Mau's brutal methods or were fearful of retribution. Others believed that British support and education were the keys to building a successful Kenya. Loyalists served as translators, sources of information and in military and police forces.

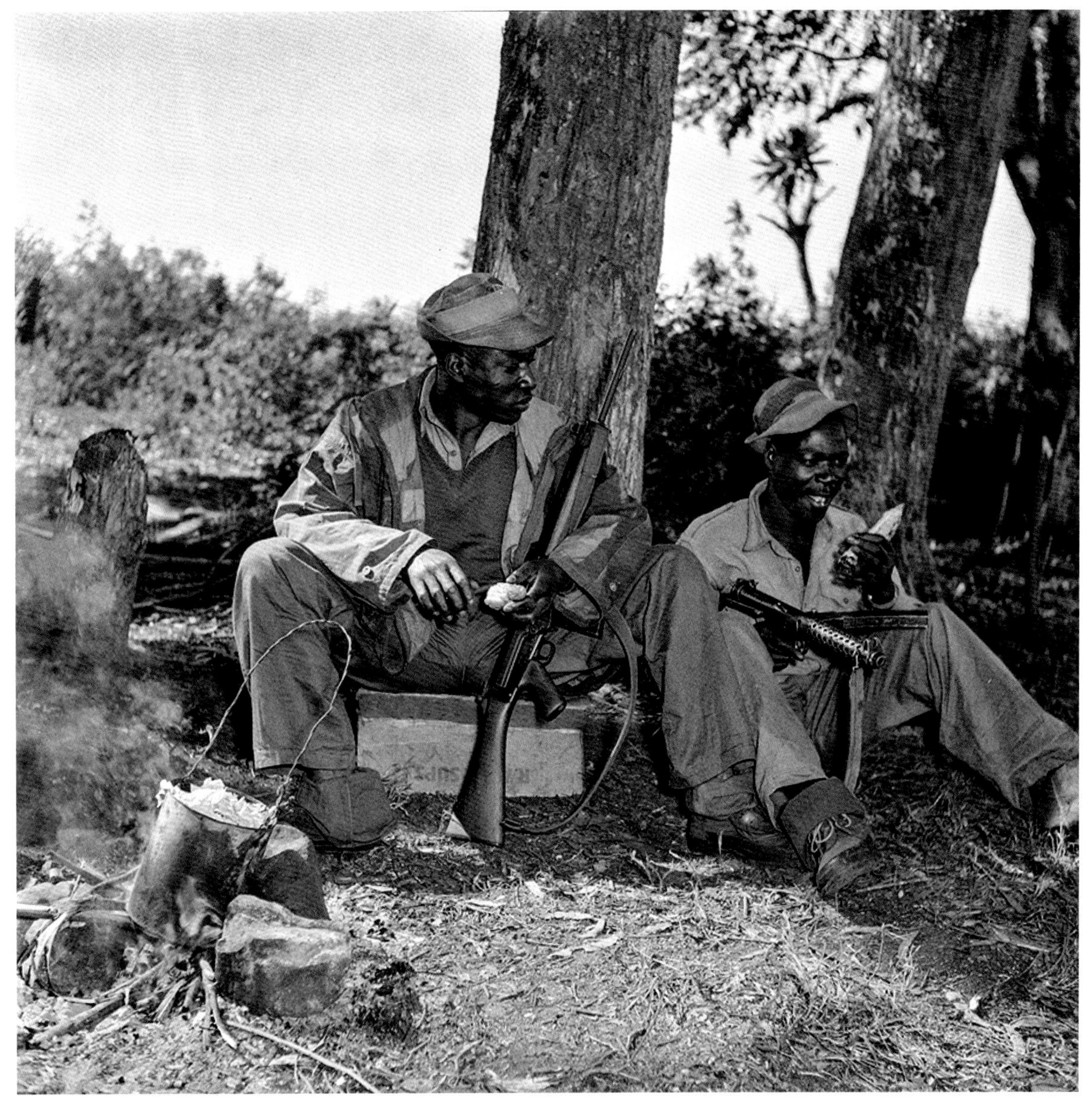

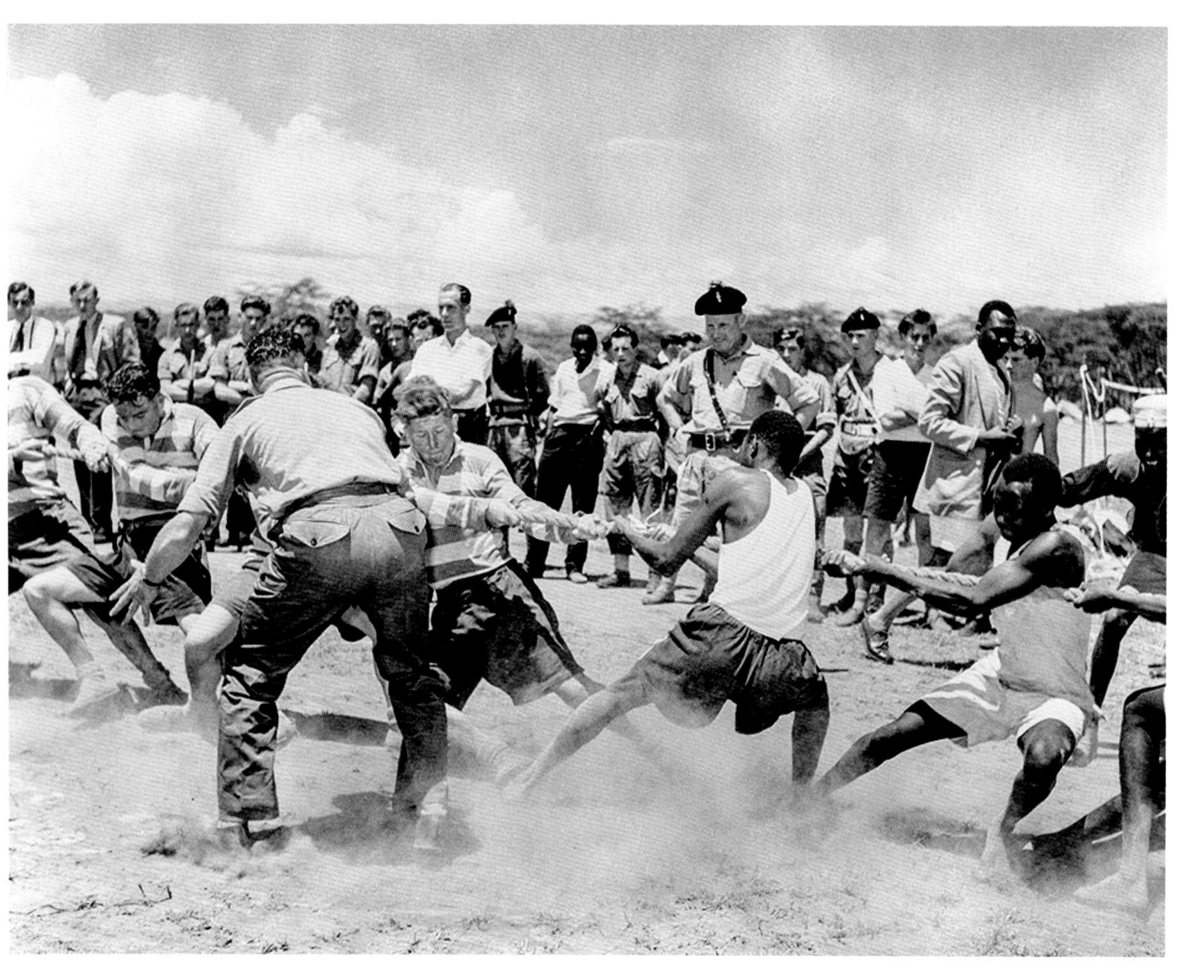

British troops and loyalist members of the Home Guard take part in a tug-of-war. Members of the Home Guard were drawn from many Kenyan communities, including those that also contained Mau Mau supporters, in particular the Kikuyu. Loyalty was rewarded by the colonial authorities, for example, with allocations of land or jobs. When Kenya moved towards self-government, loyalists controlled most of the key positions in business and politics.

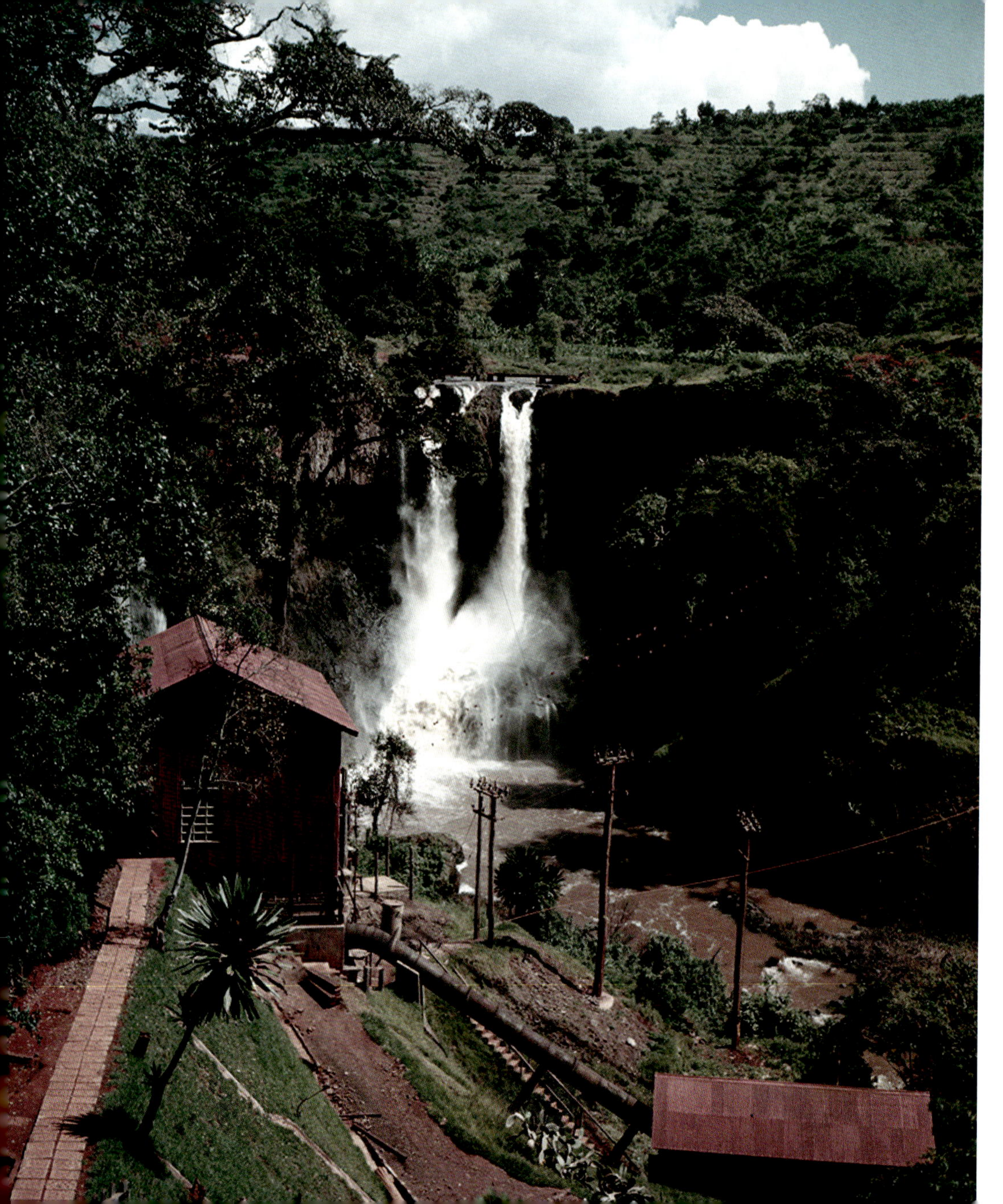

The Nyeri hydro-electric plant, 1952. The colonial authorities pushed to develop the Kenyan agricultural economy in the 1950s, in part as a response to Mau Mau. However, for Kenyan communities, land was more than simply an economic resource to be exploited. It was a vital foundation of identity and social order. Passed down through generations, land symbolised continuity and belonging: a vital link between the living and their ancestors.

Esther Muthoni was raped by soldiers before her family was moved into a colonial village in Kenya. Interviewed in 2025, she remembered: 'The British soldiers would be dropped off by trucks and they would march towards the villages on foot, if they came across a woman or child, they just attacked and raped them. In the village they found me. I was taking care of my younger siblings, they were babies, I couldn't leave them and I couldn't defend myself, it wasn't just one of them, they were many. So I just stayed, and let them "take" me so I could take care of the children. What choice did we have? We had to be strong and go through this hardship. So be strong, you take the beating and let them do what they want to do and then survive, don't die.'

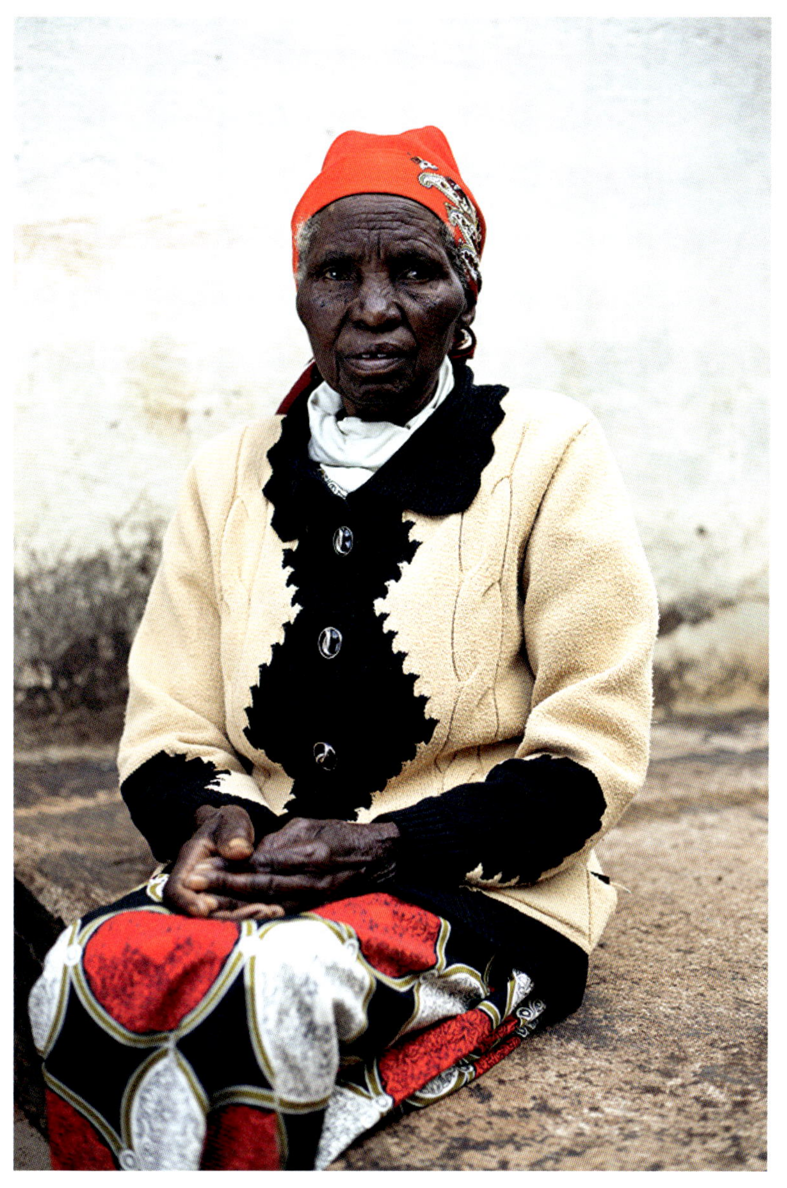

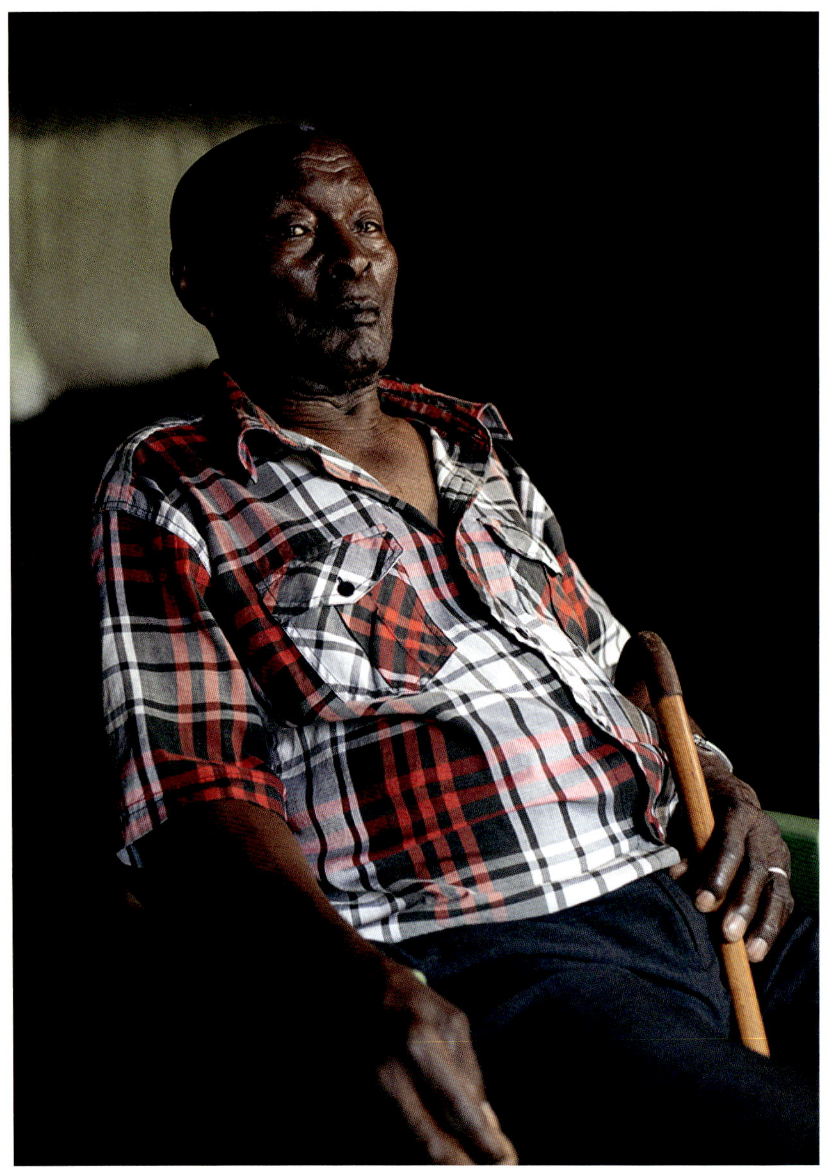

Samuel Waruinge was arrested and tortured during the Kenya 'Emergency'. 'They lit a fire in the guard quarters and for hours they beat us over and over again, interrogating us even though we did not know anything,' he remembered. 'We experienced so many problems even to this day in my old age, my legs ache I can't move as well as I would like to. It was torture. They would imprison you for no reason, while innocent. I was arrested in Nairobi, taken to Naivasha and detained for six months.'

Hannah Wanjikũ was sexually assaulted by a soldier during the Kenya 'Emergency'. 'On that day, he ordered my mother outside the house and demanded I stay behind to open a storage box. I couldn't refuse as he had a firearm,' she described in 2025. In 2013, the British government agreed to pay £20 million in compensation to a group of around 5,000 Kenyans for their experiences during the 'emergency' – around £3,000 each. Hannah was not one of the people who received compensation.

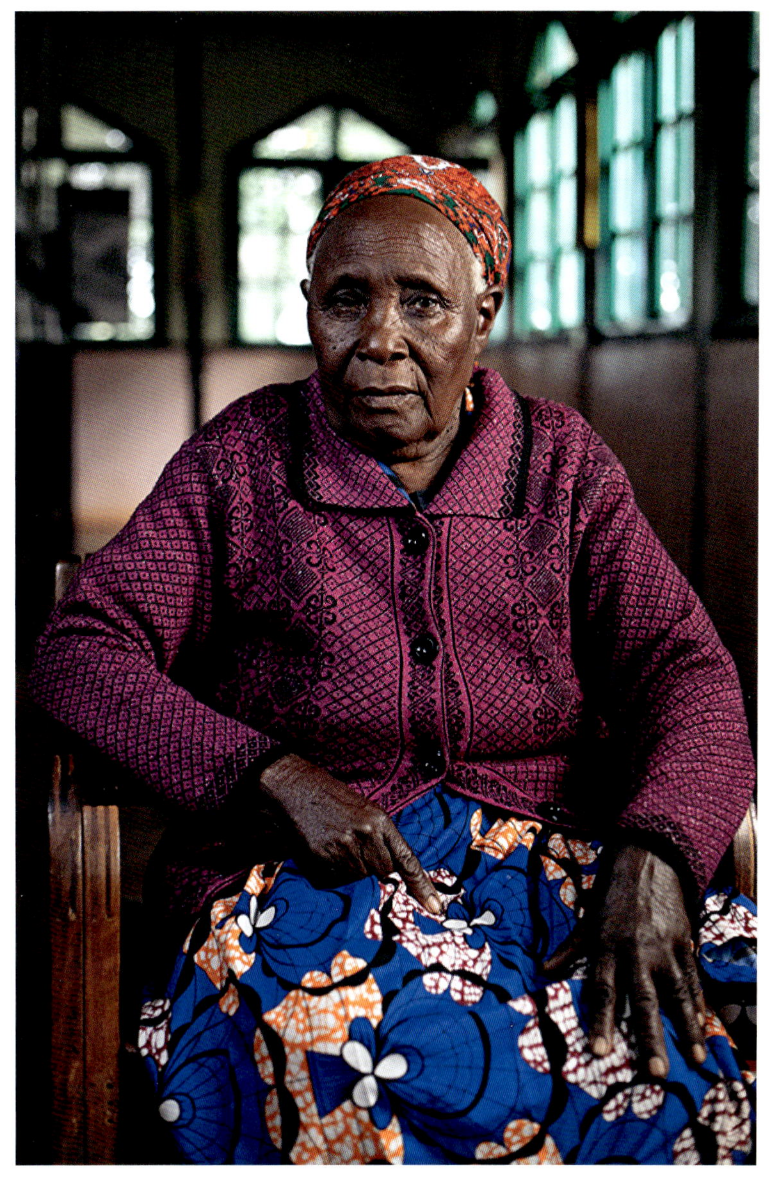

British troops get ready to return to Cyprus after the Suez campaign in 1956. Cyprus remained crucial to British foreign and defence policy. Its location enabled operations to be launched in the Middle East. The island's British military bases are used for the same purpose today.

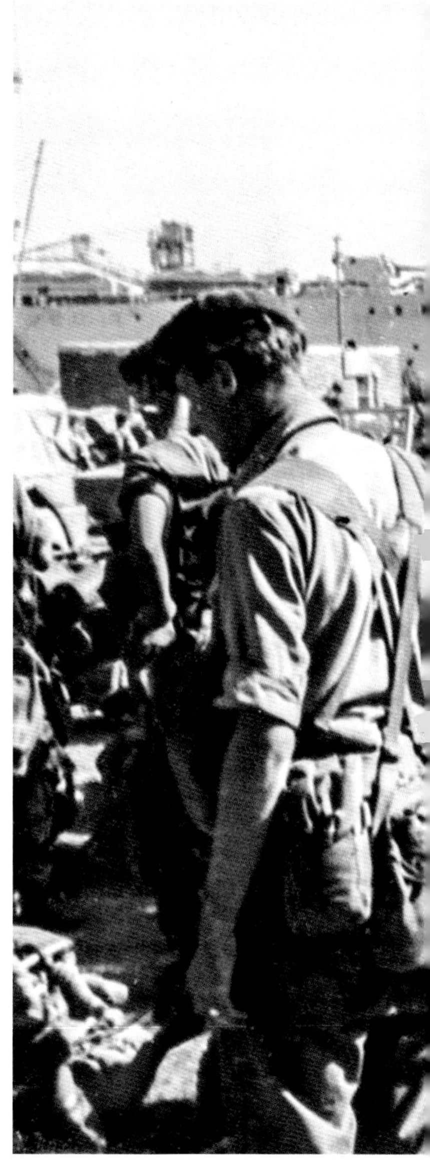

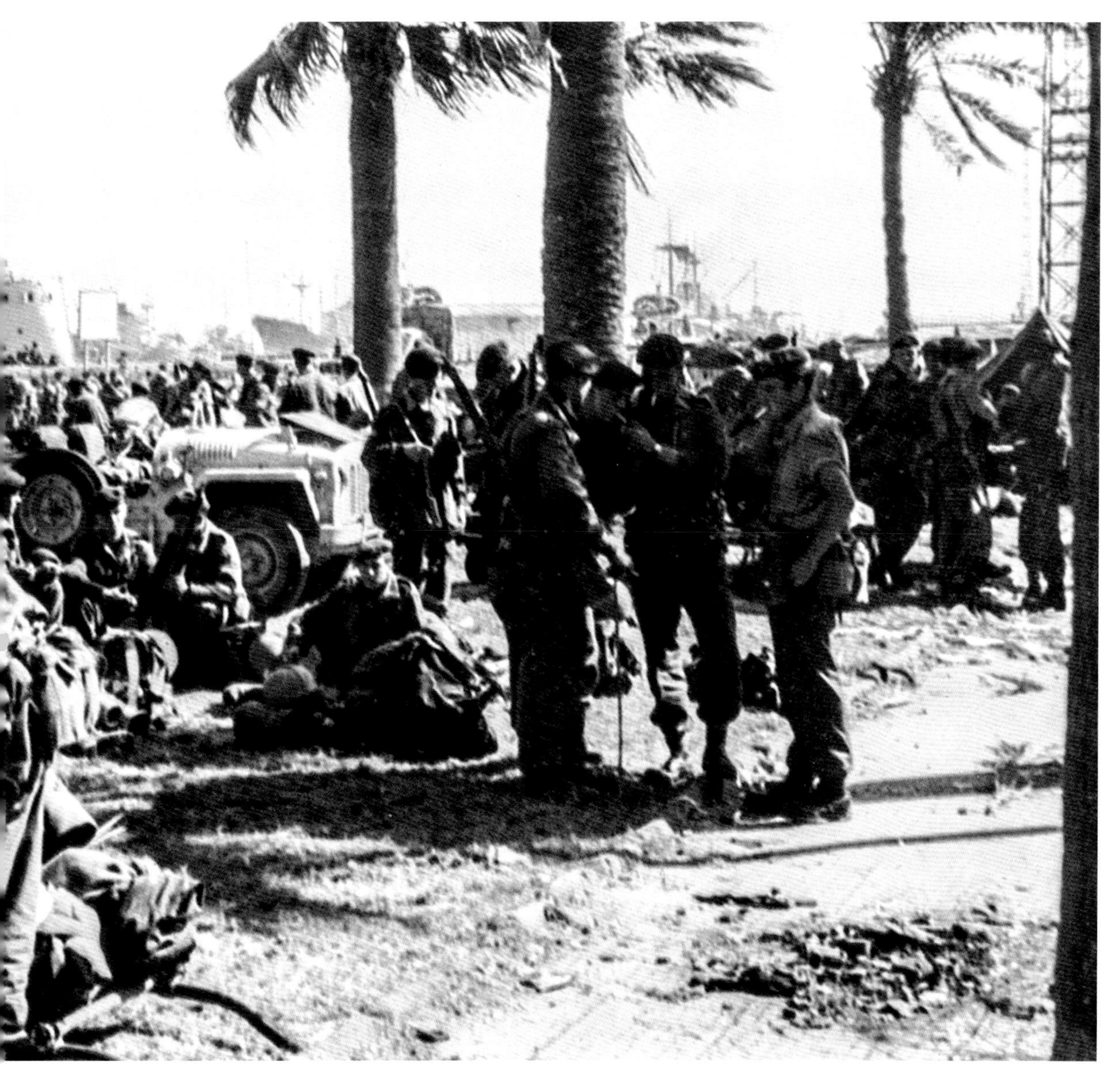

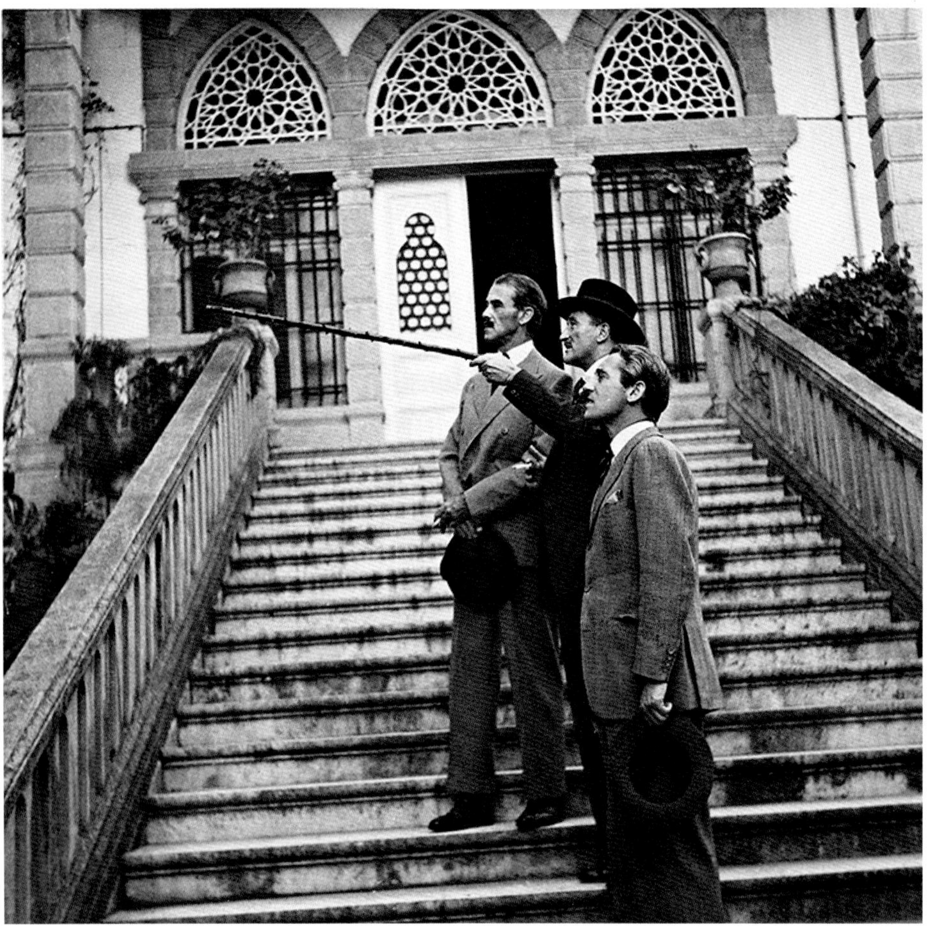

Henry Hopkinson (right) was Minister of State for Colonial Affairs. In 1954 he stated, in relation to Cyprus, that 'there are certain territories in the Commonwealth which, owing to their particular circumstances, can never expect to be fully independent.' This statement, reflecting the importance Britain attached to maintaining Cyprus as a military asset, was heavily quoted by supporters of *Enosis* (political union between Cyprus and Greece).

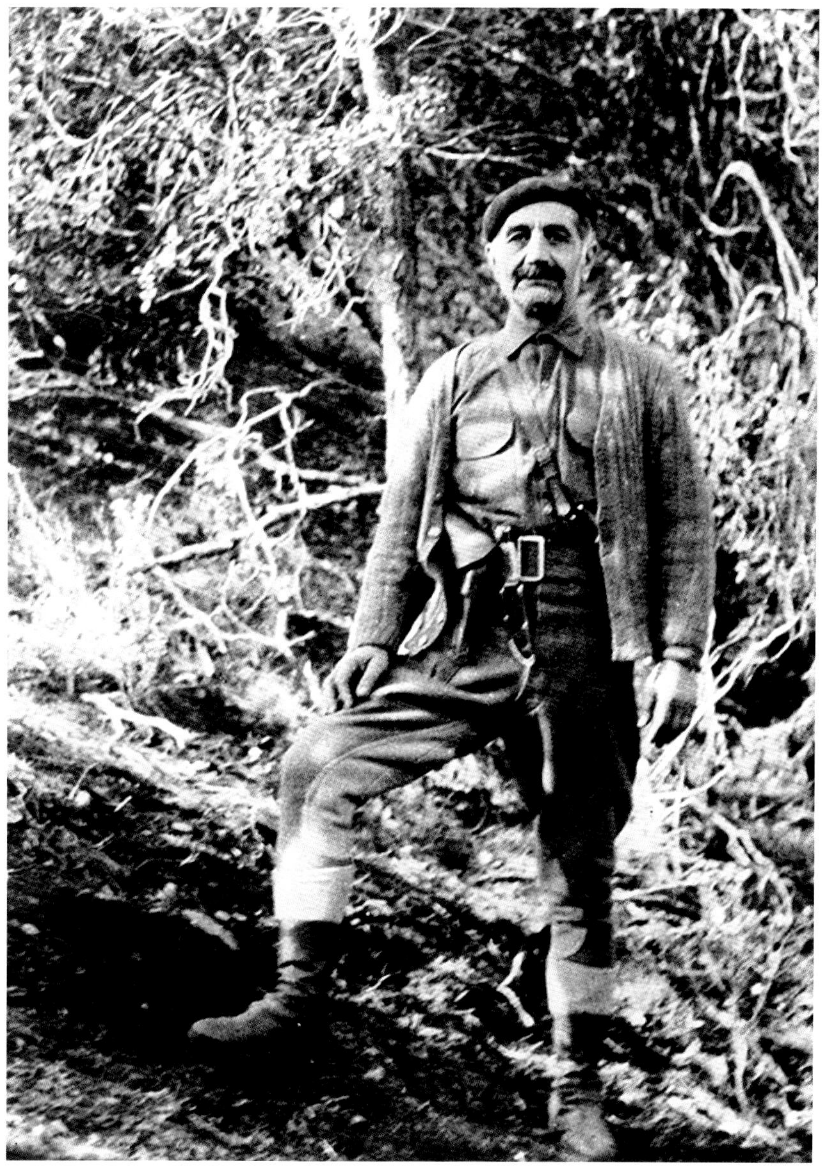

General Georgios Grivas. The political leader of the Greek Cypriot community, Archbishop Makarios III, agreed to support Grivas to lead an armed revolt. Fighters carried out sabotage and guerilla operations against British security forces and government installations. They relied on a network of supporters who supplied intelligence, weapons and hiding places. *Enosis* was hugely popular with the Greek Cypriot community, though not everyone approved of the National Organisation of Cypriot Fighters' (EOKA) methods. Civilians were often intimidated into support and 'traitors' could be killed.

A house wall painted with pro-Greek slogans in Syngrasi. EOKA and the colonial authorities battled to control the narrative: EOKA sought to emphasise support for *Enosis*, while colonial powers aimed to downplay its popularity.

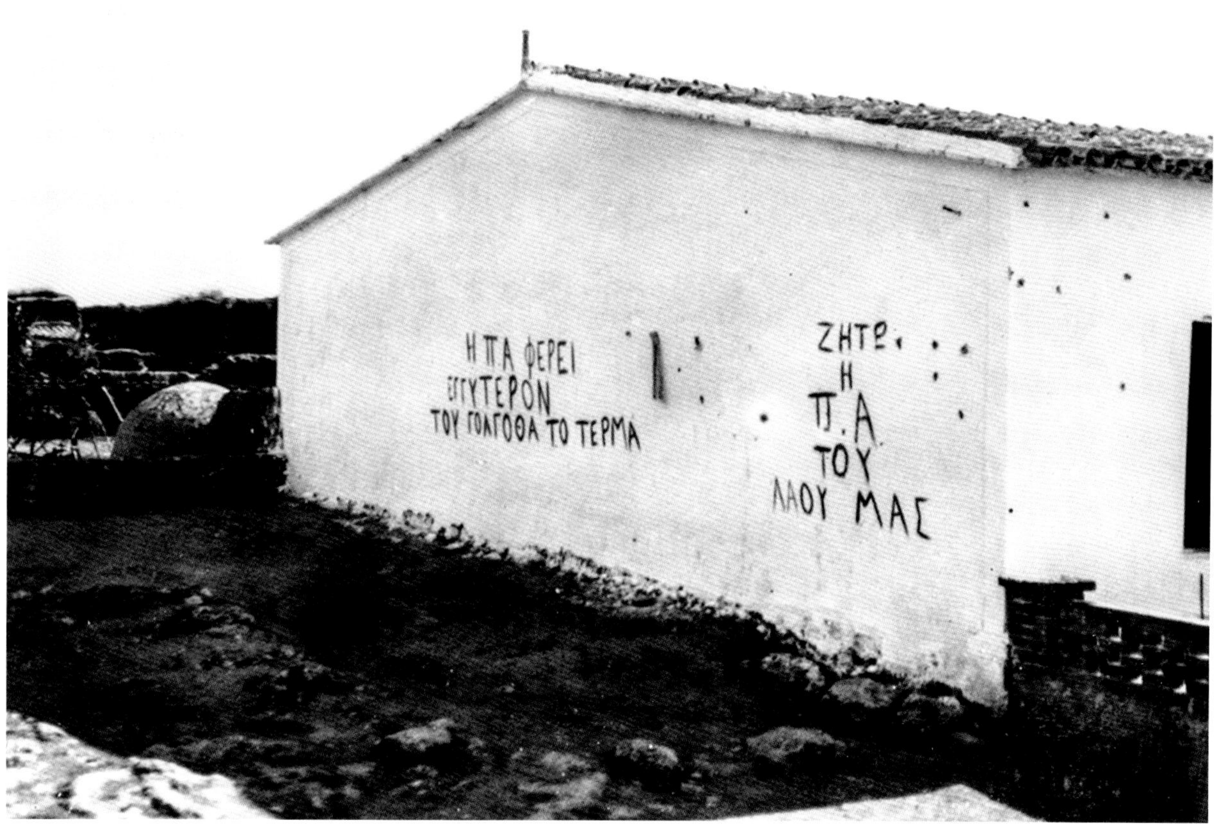
Η ΠΑ ΦΕΡΕΙ
ΕΓΓΥΤΕΡΟΝ
ΤΟΥ ΓΟΛΓΟΘΑ ΤΟ ΤΕΡΜΑ
ΖΗΤΩ
Η
Π.Α
ΤΟΥ
ΛΑΟΥ ΜΑΣ

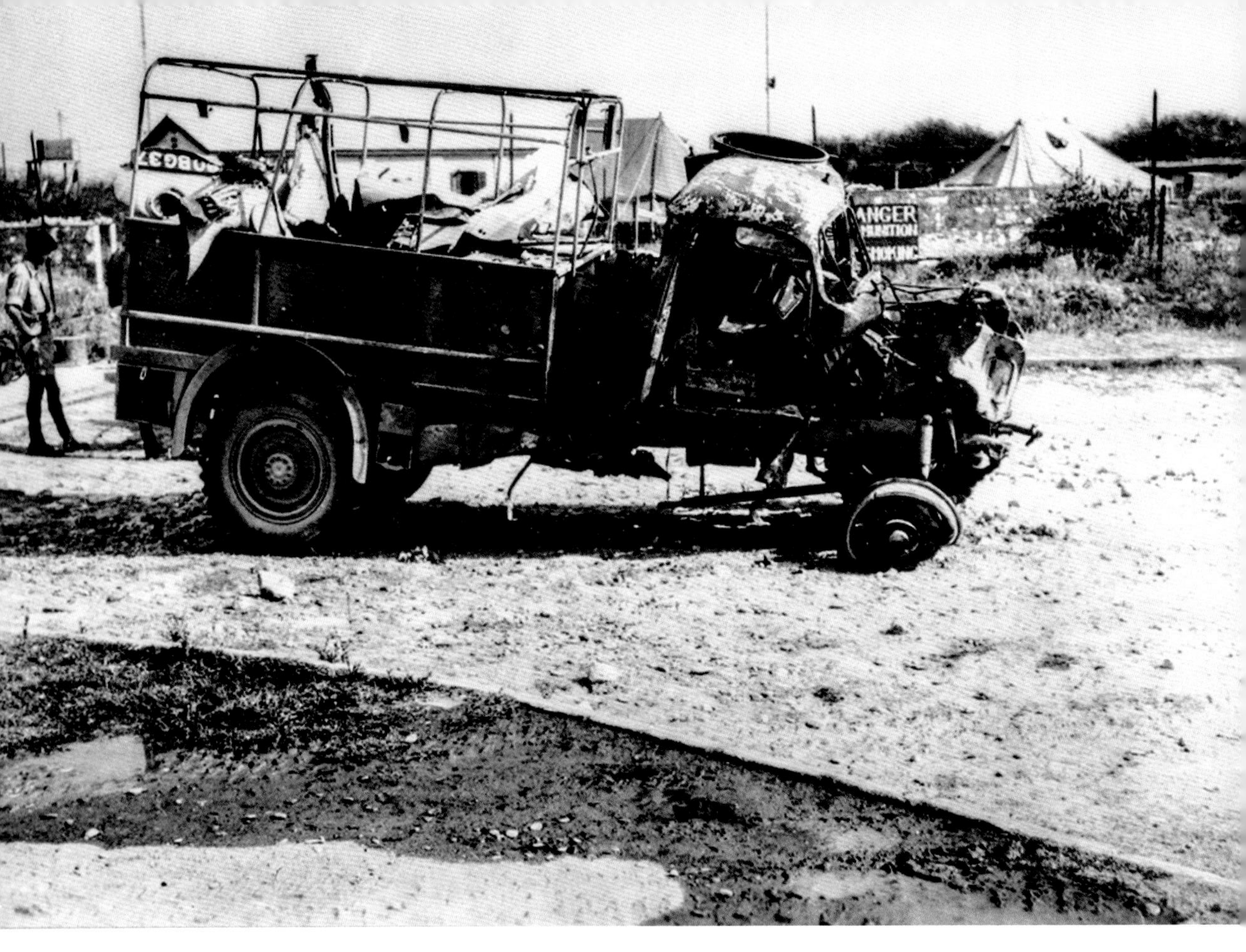
ANGER

EOKA used tactics such as sabotage and ambush to attack the much larger and better-armed British forces and Britain's colonial infrastructure. The strategy was to draw international attention to the *Enosis* cause by combining these methods with the distribution of propaganda leaflets to mobilise the local population into resistance. This photograph shows a lorry destroyed by EOKA.

The police station in the village of Lefkoniko, Cyprus. The colonial authorities – police and military – used collective punishments and other methods of control. This was designed to deter the wider population from supporting EOKA. Methods included curfews, collective fines, evictions from homes, closure of shops, the establishment of detention camps and detention without trial. Carrying items that could be used to make a bomb risked the death penalty.

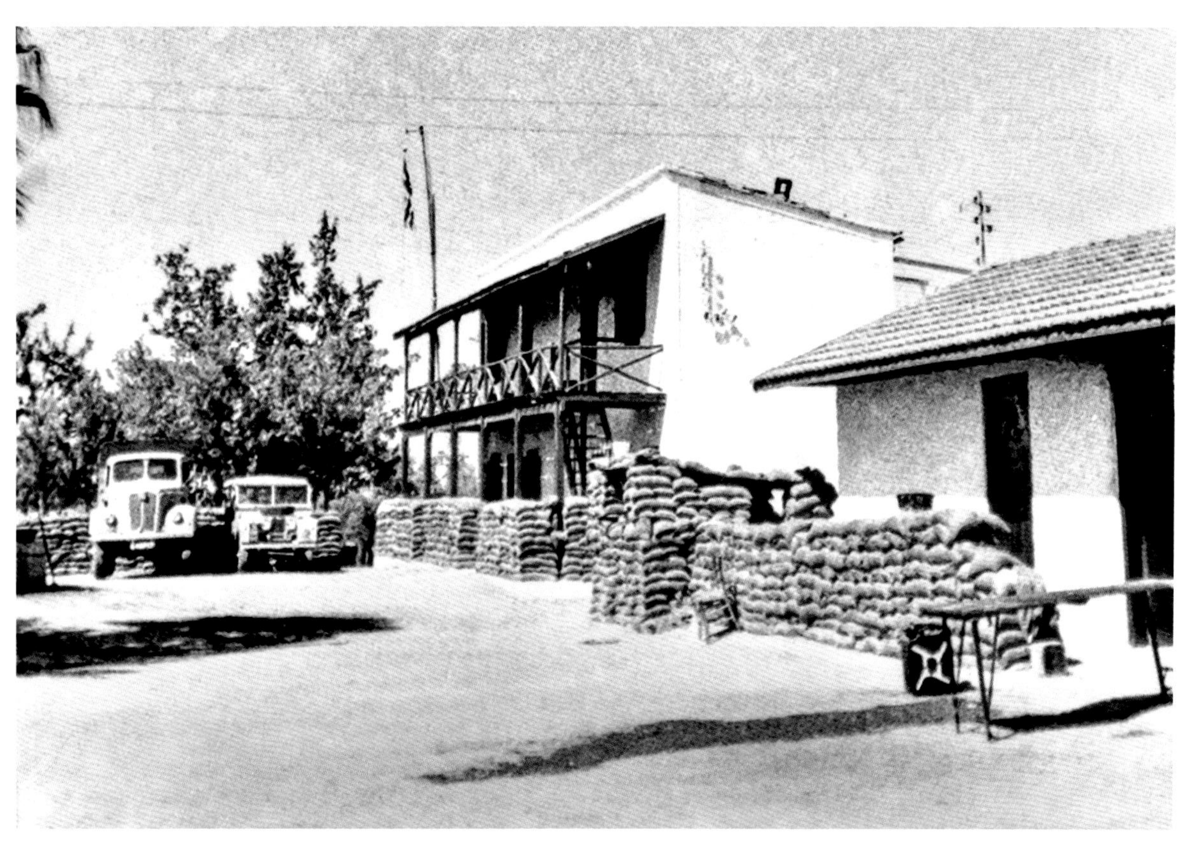

Improvised checkpoints were a common feature in Cyprus – and indeed in all three of the 'emergencies'. Identity documents, passes and permits were issued and checked regularly. This was a constant reminder of the power of the authorities, controlling where people were allowed to be, when they were allowed to be outside and who they were allowed to be with.

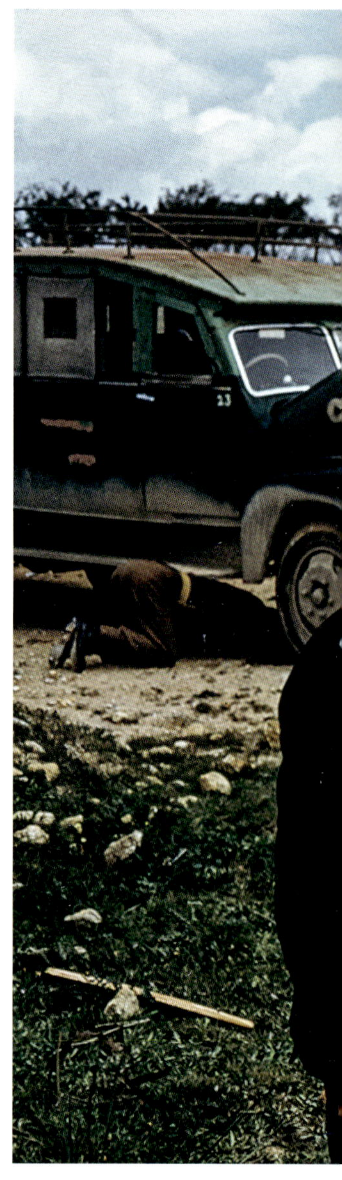

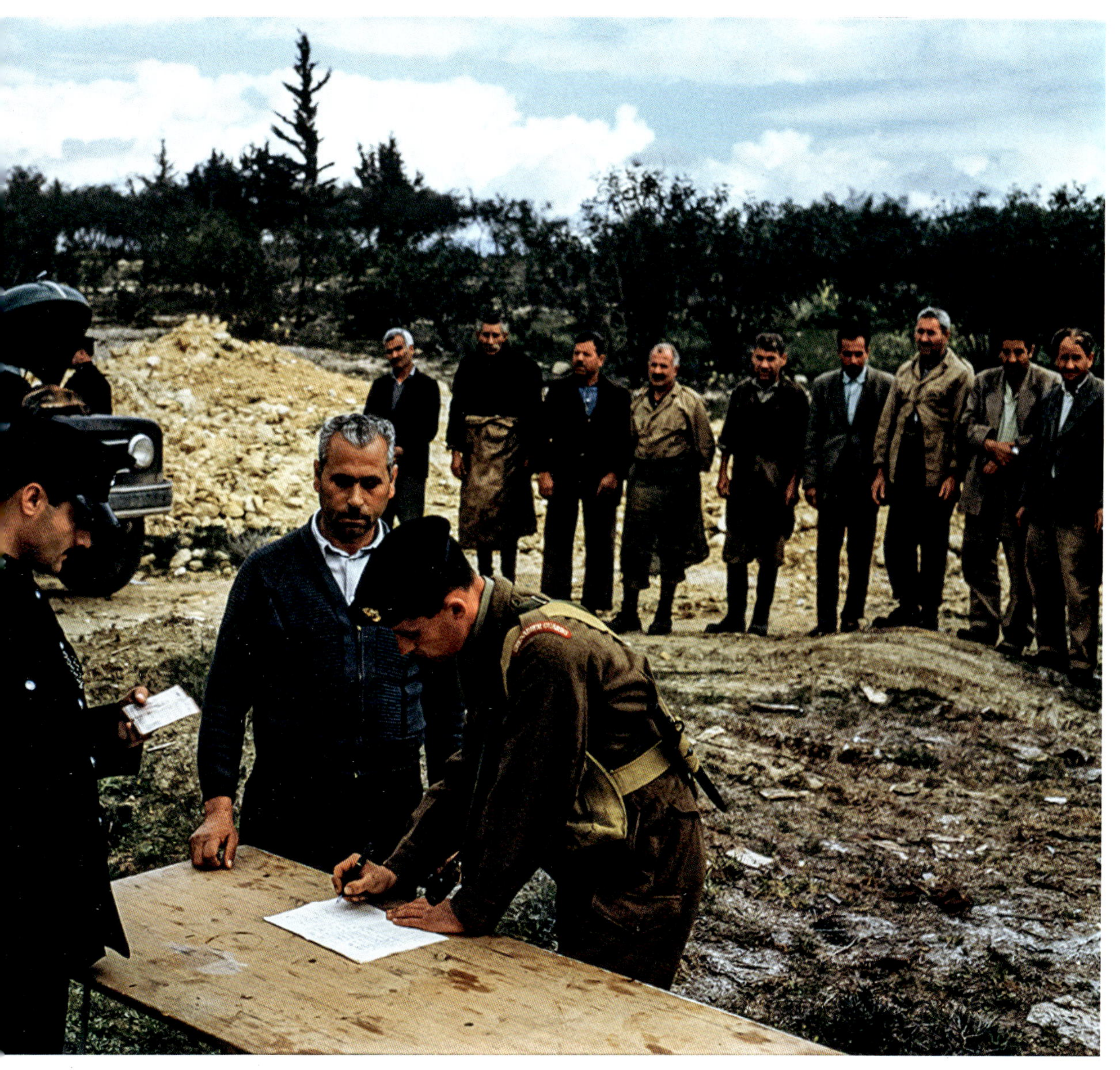

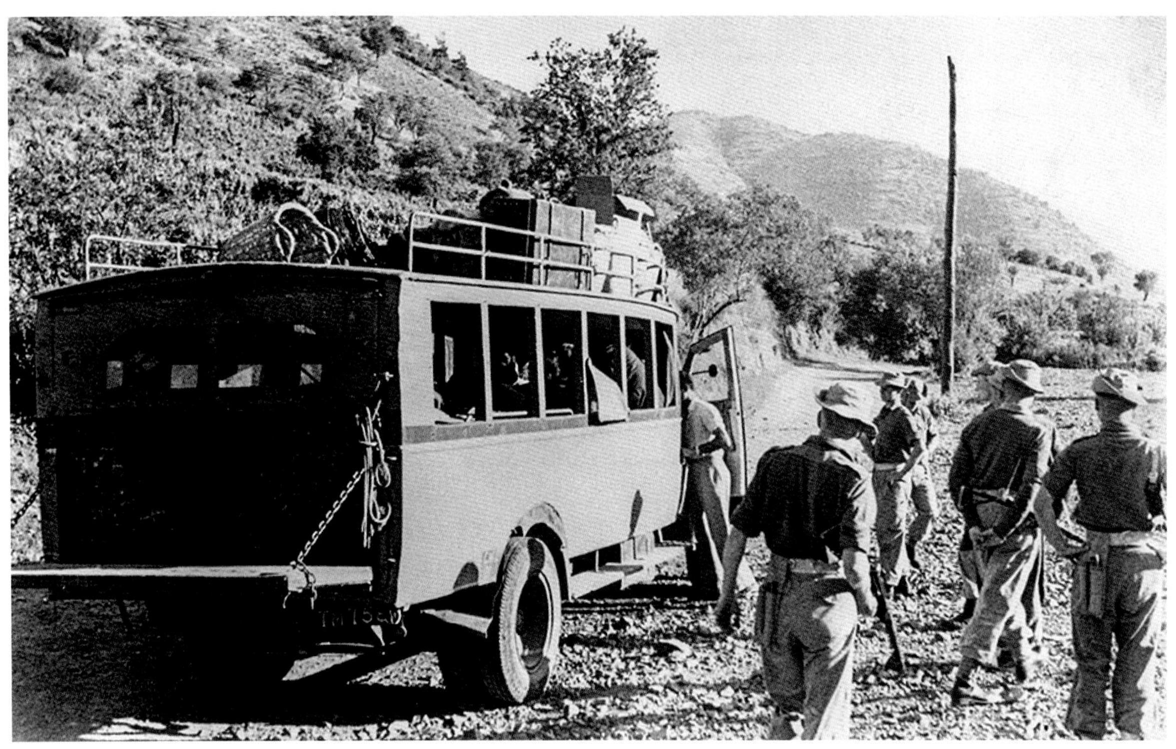

Civilians line up beside a bus as soldiers search it. The simplest and most mundane activities were disrupted, often several times per day. As frustrations boiled over and tensions rose, searches could often escalate into violence.

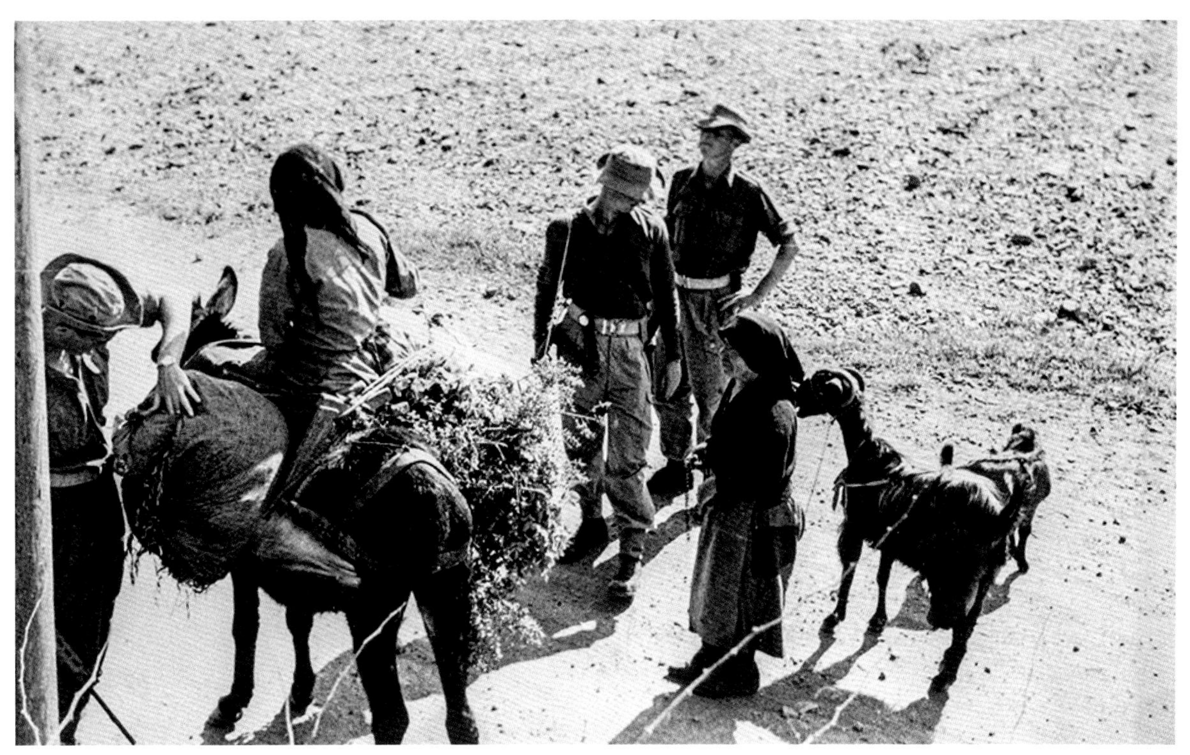

Soldiers of the Royal Ulster Rifles search loads carried on a donkey at a roadblock. For British forces, very little could be assumed to be 'neutral'. But forcing the Cypriot people to undergo such rigid controls and restrictions was often counterproductive. It helped to solidify opposition to the British and drove further support for EOKA.

'Emergency' legislation granted colonial authorities broad powers to search private homes without specific warrants or permission to track down members of EOKA or their supplies. Here a soldier of the Parachute Regiment examines a hidden door in a house in Cyprus. It led to a room in which members of EOKA were hiding. More often, searches revealed nothing.

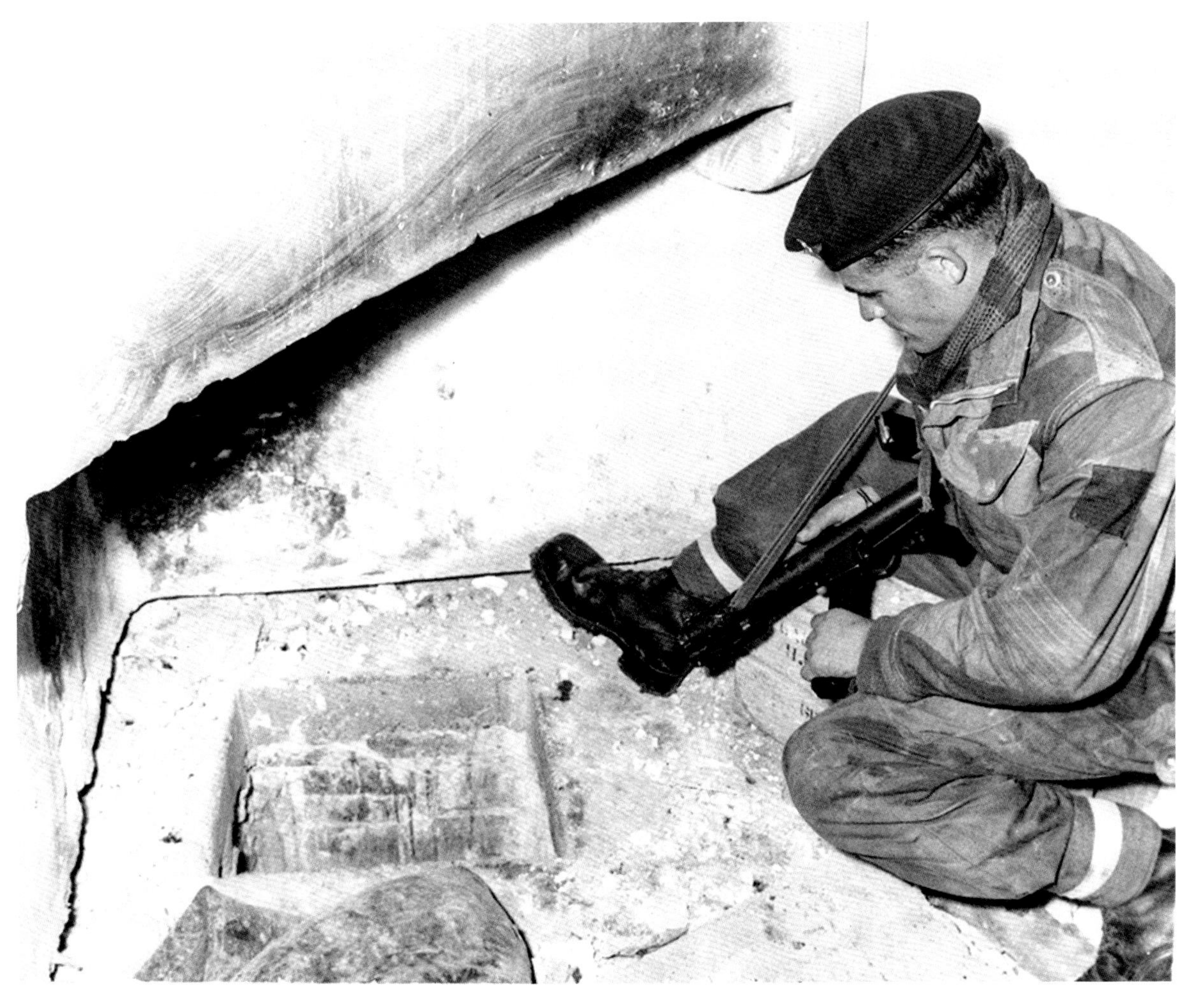

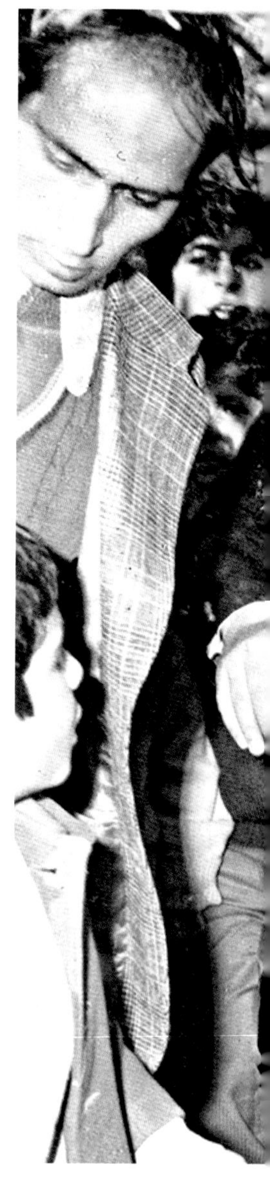

Cyprus became independent in 1960, but tensions between the Greek and Turkish communities that wanted different futures for the island grew. This social and political instability led to military conflict when Turkey invaded, causing the division of the island from 1974. Here Archbishop Makarios, a key figure in the fight for *Enosis*, visits a refugee camp at Akhna containing thousands of displaced people.

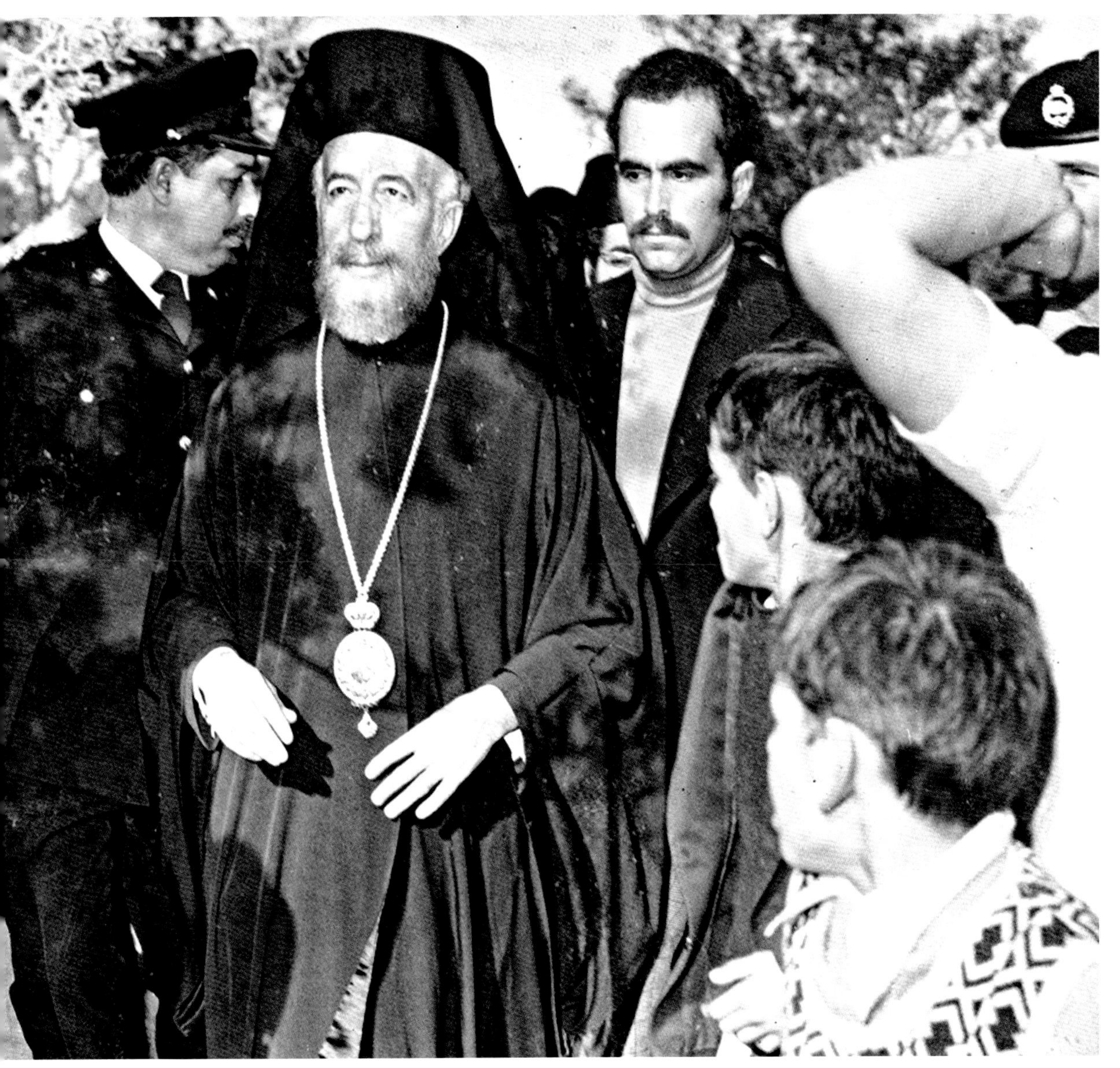

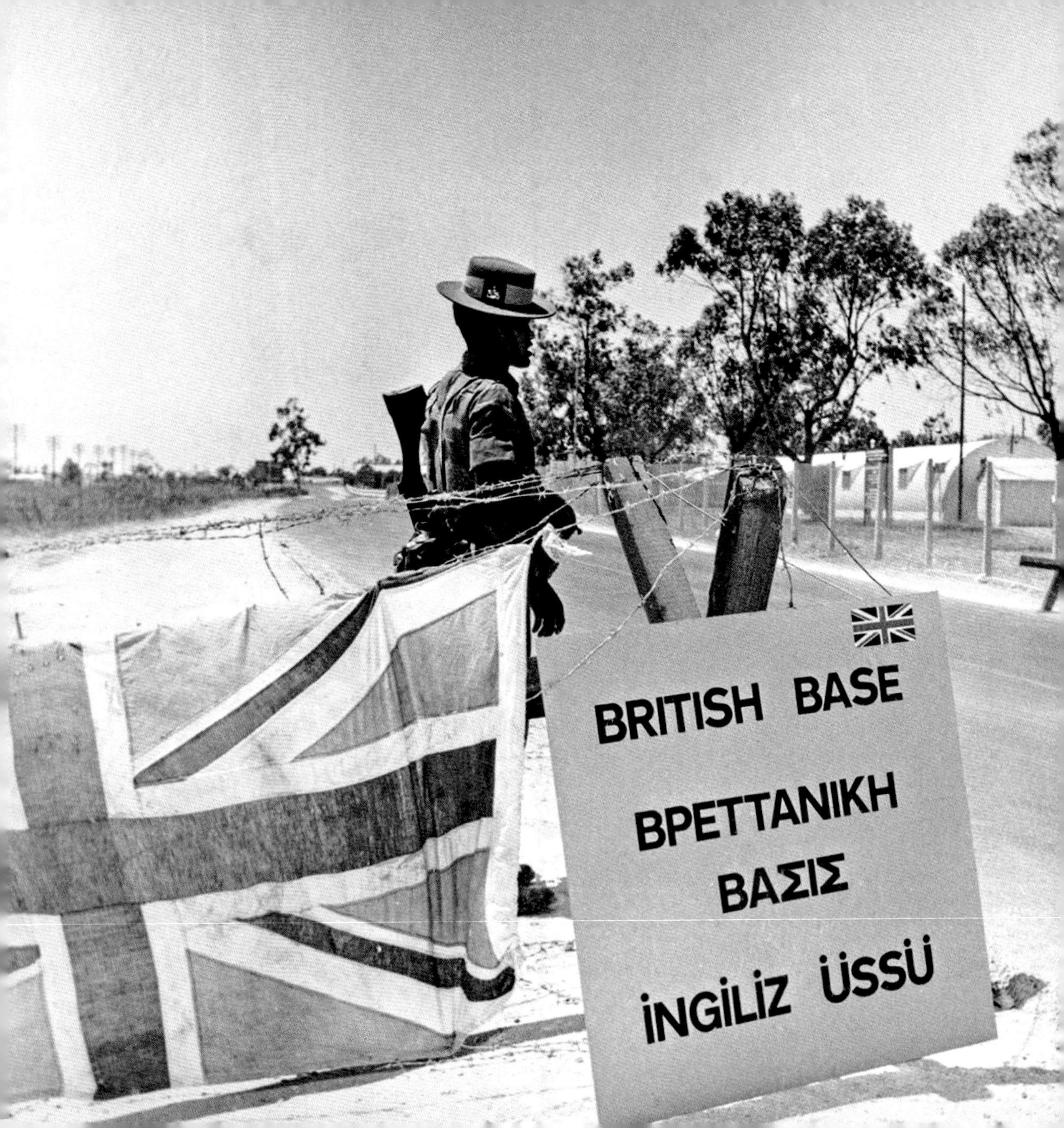
BRITISH BASE
ΒΡΕΤΤΑΝΙΚΗ
ΒΑΣΙΣ
İNGİLİZ ÜSSÜ

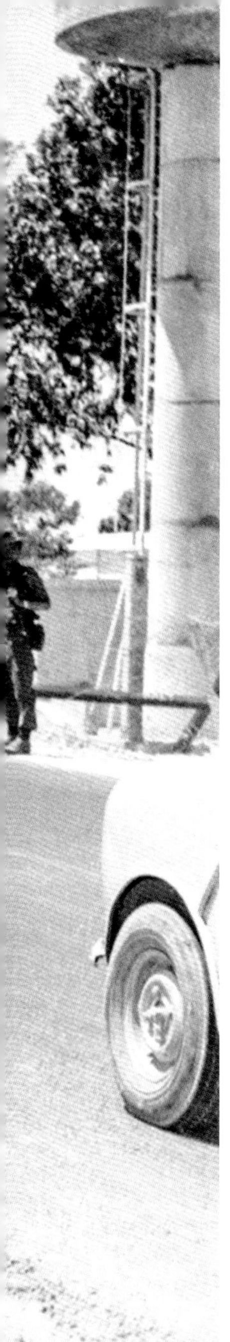

A Gurkha from The Gurkha Rifles mans a roadblock on the edge of the ESBA (Eastern Sovereign Base Area) during the 1974 Turkish invasion. Parts of Cyprus remain sovereign British territory. British forces continue to deploy from bases in Cyprus, most recently in conflicts in the Middle East and in humanitarian operations in the Mediterranean.

Image List

K 18004, Art.IWM PST 15784, PST 3112, MH 30186, SE 5979, HU 87261 © The rights holder, E 31969, GOV 4208, MAL 301, K 13972, D 88057, K 13811, K 13790, K 18004, D 88041, BF 10373, D 87941, A 32793, GOV 2667, K 13998, GOV 3830, DSC05058 © IWM, DSC05761 © IWM, BF 10946, MAU 628, MH 4600, BF 10957, HU 105532 © The rights holder, BF 10956, MAU 552, MAU 865, MAU 685, MAU 866, TR 5346, MG_7875 © IWM, MG_8159 © IWM, MG_7898 © IWM, HU 4145 © The rights holder, © Crown.IWM E 20136, © Crown.IWM CPF 130, CYP 12 © The rights holder, CYP 19 © The rights holder, CYP 1 © The rights holder, © Crown.IWM CT 32, HU 52031, HU 52033, © Crown.IWM HU 68967, © Crown. IWM MH 33858, © Crown. IWM MH 33822.

Sources

John E Flint, *Cecil Rhodes* (Boston: Little Brown, 1974)

'A Speech by His Majesty the King at the State Banquet, Kenya,' The Royal Family, 31 October 31 2023

'"They Were Horribly Wounded; I Shot Them Both Dead": Neal Ascherson Tries to Make Sense of a Traumatic Wartime Memory', *The Herald*, 29 January 2017

Winston Churchill, *The Hinge of Fate* (London: Cassell, 1951) © The rights holder

House of Lords Debate, 27 February 1952, Hansard vol. 175, col. 302

Interview with John William Noble, 17333 © IWM

Interview with Yong Chin Huat (37486) © IWM

Interview with Qin Ah Jin (37487) © IWM

Interview with Esther Muthoni (37477) © IWM

Interview with Samuel Waruinge (37485) © IWM

Interview with Hannah Wanjikũ (37479) © IWM

House of Commons Debate, 28 July 1954, Hansard, vol. 531, col. 508

About the Author

Carl Warner is Principal Curator at IWM. He has curated and authored several permanent and temporary exhibitions at IWM, including the American Air Museum at IWM Duxford and *What Remains* at IWM London. He was also lead curator for *Emergency Exits* at IWM London. He has co-authored books on the history of aviation, US army air forces in the UK, and edited for publication the diary of RAF chaplain Guy Mayfield.

Acknowledgements

The author would like to thank the fantastic team that worked on the *Emergency Exits* exhibition – curators, consultants, interviewees, participants and designers. Special thanks to Emma Booth and Megan Joyce for their diligence and super-human dedication, and to Niels Boender, Chao Maina, Rose Miyonga, Tan Teng Phee and Jeremy Taylor for their ideas, inspiration and knowledge. Final thanks to the infinite patience, stoicism and skill of Lara Bateman, Nathan Doherty and Paris Agar, without whom this book wouldn't exist.